Second Language Teacher Prosody

Second Language Teacher Prosody focuses on the prosodic characteristics of input in L2 Spanish classrooms.

Readers are led through descriptions and interpretations of prosodic behaviors based upon teachers' training and experience, their native or near-native speaker status, and their own comments about their teaching. The analysis culminates with several key discoveries and methodological implications with regard to didactic prosody, research design and methodology, and data interpretation. The conclusion offers future lines of research on SDS prosody including reception studies exploring the relative salience and effectiveness of prosodic cues. Educators can intentionally utilize these tools to achieve pedagogical goals.

This book will be of interest to scholars in Applied Linguistics and Instructed Second Language Acquisition.

Emily Kuder is Visiting Assistant Professor of Hispanic Studies at Connecticut College, USA. Dr. Kuder specializes in phonetics and phonology, particularly suprasegmental analysis, as well as second language teaching and learning. She received her PhD from the University of Wisconsin-Madison in 2017 and is author of a forthcoming article entitled "Rhetorical Stress in Spanish Second Language Classroom Instruction" to be published in *Hispania*. Dr. Kuder has also authored a chapter in the fifth edition of "Teaching Students with Language and Communication Disabilities" by Dr. Sydney Jay Kuder and is co-author of "Research on Heritage Spanish Phonetics and Phonology: Pedagogical and Curricular Implications" with Dr. Rajiv Rao published in the *Journal of New Approaches in Educational Research*.

Second Language Teacher Prosody

Emily Kuder
Spanish List Advisor: Javier Muñoz-Basols

LONDON AND NEW YORK

First published 2020 by Routledge

2 Park Square, Milton Park, Abingdon, Oxon OX14 4RN
605 Third Avenue, New York, NY 10017

Routledge is an imprint of the Taylor & Francis Group, an informa business

First issued in paperback 2021

© 2020 Emily Kuder

The right of Emily Kuder to be identified as author of this work has been asserted by her in accordance with sections 77 and 78 of the Copyright, Designs and Patents Act 1988.

All rights reserved. No part of this book may be reprinted or reproduced or utilized in any form or by any electronic, mechanical, or other means, now known or hereafter invented, including photocopying and recording, or in any information storage or retrieval system, without permission in writing from the publishers.

Notice:
Product or corporate names may be trademarks or registered trademarks, and are used only for identification and explanation without intent to infringe.

Publisher's Note
The publisher has gone to great lengths to ensure the quality of this reprint but points out that some imperfections in the original copies may be apparent.

British Library Cataloguing-in-Publication Data
A catalogue record for this book is available from the British Library

Library of Congress Cataloging-in-Publication Data
Names: Kuder, Emily, author.
Title: Second language teacher prosody / Emily Kuder.
Description: 1. | New York : Routledge, 2019. | Includes bibliographical references and index.
Identifiers: LCCN 2019036230 (print) | LCCN 2019036231 (ebook) | ISBN 9780367277871 (hardback) | ISBN 9780429297861 (ebook)
Subjects: LCSH: Spanish language–Intonation. | Spanish language–Study and teaching.
Classification: LCC PC4139.5 .K83 2019 (print) | LCC PC4139.5 (ebook) | DDC 461/.6–dc23
LC record available at https://lccn.loc.gov/2019036230
LC ebook record available at https://lccn.loc.gov/2019036231

ISBN: 978-0-367-27787-1 (hbk)
ISBN: 978-1-03-217665-9 (pbk)
DOI: 10.4324/9780429297861

Typeset in Times New Roman
by Wearset Ltd, Boldon, Tyne and Wear

Contents

List of illustrations vii

1 **The garnish to our words** 1

   Introduction 1
   Prosody during student-directed speech 2
   Overview of contents 5

2 **Directing attention** 8

   Introduction 8
   Prosodic prominence 9
   Acoustic correlates of stress and focus 13
   Speech melody 17

3 **Didactic speech accommodation and modification** 29

   Introduction 29
   Formal and informal speech 29
   Second language classroom discourse 33
   Second language teacher variation 37
   Accommodative speech styles and contexts 39

4 **Participants and procedures** 47

   Introduction 47
   Description of participants 49
   Data collection procedures 50
   Data input, coding, and analysis 56

5 Prosodic correlates of SDS   66

Introduction 66
Articulation rate and intensity 66
Pitch mean and range 70
F0 peak frequency and pre-nuclear F0 rise pattern 74
Boundary pitch movement 79

6 Individual differences and prosodic changes over time   86

Introduction 86
Prosodic variation across TAs 87
Changes over the academic semester 91

7 Conclusions, implications, and future research   101

Introduction 101
Conclusions 101
Implications of the findings 105
Future research directions 108

Index   112

Illustrations

Figures

2.1	Broad focus versus contrastive focus intonation	16
2.2	Broad focus declarative intonation	20
3.1	F0 suppression in conversation	31
3.2	Speech elicitation tasks	33
4.1	BPM shapes	59
5.1	Intensity contours in SDS and conversation	67
5.2	Articulation rate in SDS and conversation	68
5.3	Mean intensity in SDS and conversation	68
5.4	Pitch contours in SDS and conversation	71
5.5	F0 mean in SDS and conversation	72
5.6	F0 range in SDS and conversation	72
5.7	Pitch contour in SDS	75
5.8	Pitch contour in conversation	75
5.9	F0 peaks per second in SDS and conversation	76
5.10	BPM frequency in SDS and conversation	79
5.11	Pitch contour showing BPM in SDS and conversation	79
5.12	BPM shapes in SDS and conversation	80
5.13	Utterance purpose in SDS	81
6.1	Articulation rate by nativeness in SDS and conversation	88
6.2	Mean intensity by nativeness in SDS and conversation	88
6.3	Articulation rate across time in SDS	92
6.4	Mean intensity across time in SDS	93
6.5	F0 mean across time in SDS	93
6.6	F0 range across time in SDS	94
6.7	Overall F0 range across time in SDS	94
6.8	Alejandra's pre-nuclear F0 rise patterns across time in SDS	95
6.9	Lola's BPM across time in SDS	95

Tables

4.1	Biographical data	51
4.2	Experience and educational background	52
4.3	Curricular information	54

1 The garnish to our words

Introduction

When I first started teaching Spanish at the collegiate level, I realized quickly that when I step into the classroom, I transform instantly into a different version of myself. I act and speak differently than I do in other sectors of my life. For instance, I carefully choose the words I use, opting for more frequent terms and cognates that I deem easier for students to comprehend, I speak more slowly than usual and exaggerate particularly noteworthy words and phrases, and I use what I perceive as captivating physical and vocal gestures. My fascination with these observations grew as I matured as a teacher, and through conversations with colleagues and students I found that I am not alone. In fact, many of my behaviors are shared by other second language (L2) teachers, are noticed in some cases by L2 students, and have been documented both anecdotally and empirically through scholarly studies.

To provide an example, consider this fragment from a hypothetical intermediate-level L2 Spanish class. Imagine that Professor Cruz just introduced a two-part activity to review climate change vocabulary and practice new grammar topics, but the students gave him a confused look. He goes on to clarify the assignment in the following fashion:

> *Profesor Cruz: ¿Entienden bien la actividad? Hay que escribir unas ideas individualmente primero sobre el efecto del cambio climático y luego formar grupos de dos o tres para tener conversaciones sobre lo que escribieron. Sería mejor conversar sobre los temas en vez de simplemente leer sus respuestas individuales. Deben usar el vocabulario de la lista sobre el clima, como* **gases de efecto invernadero***, e incorporar la gramática que hemos estado repasando, en particular el subjuntivo y el futuro simple. Recuerden que se usa el subjuntivo en las expresiones de opinión, por ejemplo, "Es desastroso que el gobierno no apoye la producción de fuentes de energía limpia."*

2 *The garnish to our words*

Professor Cruz: Do you all understand the activity? You need to write ideas down individually first about the effect of climate change and then form groups of two or three in order to have conversations about what you wrote. It would be better to converse about the topics instead of simply reading your individual responses. You should use vocabulary from the list about the climate, like *greenhouse gases*, and incorporate the grammar we have been going over, in particular the subjunctive and simple future. Remember that you use subjunctive to express opinions, for instance, "It's disastrous that the government does not support the production of sources of clean energy."

Based on Professor Cruz's objectives, his speech would likely include several instances of linguistic accommodations to emphasize important vocabulary, highlight vital administrative points, and guide the listeners through the instructional discourse. He may stress the word *individualmente* 'individually' in the second sentence of his statement in order to note the two phases of the activity and instruct the students to complete an individual task prior to forming small groups. He may emphasize the word *conversar* 'to converse' to reinforce his suggestion that the students have a conversation with each other instead of reading their responses aloud to one another. He would likely slow down his speech in order to facilitate comprehension, and he would clearly enunciate target terminology such as *gases de efecto invernadero* 'greenhouse gases' and *energía limpia* 'clean energy' to model pronunciation. Professor Cruz may also lower the tone of his voice at the end of his statement in order to indicate finality and cue to the students to begin the activity. Though these accommodations are predictable, they are not systematic and vary widely from teacher to teacher.

Prosody during student-directed speech

Many of the linguistic accommodations that occur during L2 teacher talk and are observed by both teachers and students involve prosody, which includes the speed and loudness of speech as well as tonal modulations, i.e., rises and falls in vocal pitch (Chaudron, 1988). Speakers utilize prosody for a variety of purposes, such as to express emotions, to organize speech messages at the discourse level, to direct attention, and even to facilitate learning (Crystal, 2005). For this reason, although there are many vital components of the way teachers express themselves in L2 classrooms, the focus of this book is to describe the prosodic qualities of teacher talk. Prosody directly affects the speech signal produced by the speaker without necessarily influencing lexical choices. If oral speech was a plate of tacos al pastor from Mexico, prosody would be the cilantro and diced onions sprinkled on top. In other words, prosody affects speech at the suprasegmental level as it is "superimposed on vowels and consonants" as opposed to affecting segments themselves, which are represented through vocalized codes or symbols that carry linguistic information (Hualde, 2005, p. 301). In the taco analogy, the tortillas, pork, and pineapple are the sounds that make up the words forming part of the larger syntax of a statement. Those who study prosody are concerned with both its form and function, including how prosody is articulated, where emphasis is placed, and for what purposes (Wagner & Watson, 2010).

Changes in tempo, rhythm, volume, and tone all contribute to the portrayal of prominence, which is defined as increased articulatory effort often used to mark the relative importance of an utterance or piece of an utterance. However, in the L2 classroom, prominence marking is multifaceted as it is potentially influenced by a variety of factors tied to the teacher's personality, expertise, instructional strategies and objectives, teaching methods, and so on. Therefore, when considering prominence in naturally-occurring L2 classrooms, it is necessary to account for as many of these potentially intervening variables as possible. Of course, many of these factors are difficult or impossible to measure faithfully, so both quantitative and qualitative data are essential to understanding prosodic behavior. To gather quantitative information about prosody, researchers utilize acoustic visualization software such as Praat (Boersma & Weenink, 2016) through which it is possible to see oscillograms representing sound waveforms and spectrograms showing the frequencies that make up sounds. From here, extracting exact measurements of prosodic correlates is facilitated. As far as qualitative data, it is common in the fields of Instructed Second Language Acquisition (ISLA) and Applied Linguistics to use biographical questionnaires and interviews to capture the nuances of variables affecting prosody.

Even when studying prosody from multiple perspectives, the actual purpose behind prosodic manipulations and the true intentions of teachers are obscured by the complexity of discourse in L2 classrooms. L2 teachers play many roles, including serving as models of the target language (TL) while simultaneously purveying knowledge of TL structures to the students, directing the flow of conversations and interactions, managing the classroom, and leading course administration. Teacher talk, which will be referred to in this book as student-directed speech (SDS), is laced with these competing objectives that undoubtedly shape its prosodic structure (Christie, 2002; Hualde, 2007; Willis, 1992). The term SDS refers specifically to a teacher-led classroom environment and not merely any environment where teaching and learning takes place. For instance, a one-on-one teacher-student conference would not be a context for SDS, as the teacher in this case is more of a tutor, and many of the aforementioned roles of the classroom teacher are reduced or absent entirely.

The L2 classroom is an environment that breeds a unique speech style due to the multitude of usage functions, but some aspects of SDS are comparable to other speech styles that are also accommodative and presentational by nature. For instance, many have compared SDS with *motherese*, i.e., the speech of caregivers when addressing infants and children (Walsh, 2013). You may have noticed that older people tend to use an extraordinarily high pitch register and modulate their tone to extremes when speaking to young children, and children seem to be engaged for the most part by this captivating style. Similarly, when speaking with someone who is not a proficient speaker of the language being used, you may find yourself speaking louder and slower and using more common words. These accommodation strategies are not learned, but rather happen intuitively based on the context of the conversation. In presentational speech styles such as news broadcasts, lectures like TED Talks, speeches, and radio programs, speakers tend to articulate loudly and clearly and use exaggerated prosody to express emotions and mark the continuation or the end of an idea, for example (Crystal, 2005). All these examples elucidate the prosodic changes that occur as a result of the social interaction taking place.

Focusing on the L2 classroom, it is both challenging and important to detangle pedagogical function of SDS prosody from pragmatic usage when determining consequences on learning and implications for teaching. Based on informal discussions with L2 students, it is evident that many are aware that their teachers are slowing down their speech and using formal grammar, and these accommodations are typically perceived as useful. One student commented that their El Salvadoran teacher slowed down their speech and enunciated a lot, which that student perceived as beneficial to their comprehension. However, several students noted that these adjustments seem to depend on the proficiency level of the students, suggesting that teachers use slower speech with less advanced students. Similarly, students commented that course level is an important consideration in this discussion, as using extra gestures, repeating key points, slowing down speech, and choosing "easier" words are valuable tools for teachers to use in beginner-level classes. Finally, students also mentioned attention as a relevant factor in teaching style, commenting that sometimes particular styles attract the attention of otherwise disinterested students, despite the potential pedagogical reasons for stylistic accommodations.

Although many students notice prosodic modifications during SDS, the effect of these modifications on students remains unknown. There is little research on whether particular components of SDS are beneficial or harmful to the learning process. It is also possible that the effect is variable depending on the individual learner, or even that there is no discernible pedagogical consequence. After speaking with students, it is clear that students themselves are undecided as to the effect of teacher talk on their own learning. While some say that a teacher's slower speech rate aids in oral comprehension, others find a slow pace annoying, distracting, or hindering. For instance, in advanced-level courses, students feel that exposure to "natural" speech is imperative as it is more difficult to practice advanced listening and speaking skills through other resources like textbooks and language learning applications. One student commented that hearing more natural speech during class facilitates their learning, claiming that their exposure to more fluid language has prepared them more for "real life." Other students agree that listening to swift speech helps them learn even if they don't necessarily understand every word. These viewpoints are substantiated by a particularly perceptive student who commented that they find it easier to understand "Professor Spanish" compared to listening to other speakers, possibly due to their lack of exposure to the swift speech rate that occurs in language settings beyond the classroom. Although anecdotes from students about their perspectives are informative, a clearer picture of prosodic qualities of SDS would provide an empirical basis for perception studies on learning.

Furthermore, there is great interest in the development of L2 oral proficiency, and there is considerable evidence that immersing oneself in an environment where the TL is the dominant language of use, such as through a study abroad program, leads to greater gains in pronunciation (Avello & Lara, 2014; Muñoz & Llanes, 2014). From a purely speculative standpoint, it is possible that the differential effects of learning context on L2 pronunciation development are at least in part influenced by the linguistic accommodations that occur in SDS. If this is the case, then teachers may be able to bridge this gap through materials development and further professional training. Regardless, the association between learning context and L2 pronunciation development necessitates a more in-depth exploration into the effect of exposure to didactic input on the learning experience of students. The first step in that process is to gain a comprehensive understanding of the prosodic qualities of SDS itself.

Overview of contents

The main goal of this book is to describe SDS prosody as it occurs in naturally-occurring L2 classrooms, including a detailed exploration of prosodic variation across teachers and over time. The research that forms the backbone of the analyses and discussions presented here involves naturalistic speech sampling and a mixed-methods design that sheds light on how prosodic realizations vary according to individual characteristics of teachers such as status as native speakers (NSs) or near-native speakers (NNSs), personality and teaching methods, general education and teacher training, and prior experience in the classroom. The level of familiarity between students and teachers is also explored as a possible influence on prosodic behavior. Quantitative data is analyzed from a critical standpoint to develop informed interpretations and conclusions about the speech style, and the results have implications regarding L2 pedagogy and research methodology.

Chapters 2 and 3 lay the groundwork for the discussion of linguistic evidence presented in this book by defining key concepts related to prosodic prominence, exploring previous scholarly studies on prosody and variation, and describing prosody during L2 classroom discourse and in other similar speech styles. Chapter 4 then introduces the primary research offered in this book including the overarching methodological framework, research questions, recruitment and data collection procedures, and steps taken during data extraction, coding, and analysis. Chapters 5 and 6 present quantitative findings based on descriptive and statistical analyses and provide a series of interpretations according to background questionnaires and one-on-one interviews with the teachers. Finally, Chapter 7 outlines the main conclusions drawn, discusses both pedagogical and methodological implications of the findings, and proposes future lines of research.

References

Avello, P., & Lara, A. R. (2014). Phonological development in L2 speech production during study abroad programmes differing in length of stay. In C. Pérez-Vidal (Ed.), *Language acquisition in study abroad and formal instruction contexts* (pp. 137–166). PA: John Benjamins. doi: 10.1075/aals.13.08ch6

Boersma, P., & Weenink, D. (2016). *Praat: Doing phonetics by computer [computer program]*, Version 6.0.19. Retrieved from www.praat.org/

Chaudron, C. (1988). Teacher talk in second-language classrooms. In C. Chaudron (Ed.), *Second language classrooms* (pp. 50–89). Cambridge: Cambridge University Press. doi: 10.1017/CBO9781139524469.005

Christie, F. (2002). *Classroom discourse analysis: A functional perspective*. London: Bloomsbury Publishing. doi: 10.1590/S0102-44502006000100012

Crystal, D. (2005). *How language works: How babies babble, words change meaning, and languages live or die*. New York, NY: Avery.

Hualde, J. I. (2005). *The sounds of Spanish*. Cambridge: Cambridge University Press. doi: 10.1017/CBO9780511719943

Hualde, J. I. (2007). Stress removal and stress addition in Spanish. *Journal of Portuguese Linguistics*, 59–89. doi: 10.5334/jpl.145

Muñoz, C. & Llanes, À. (2014). Study abroad and changes in degree of foreign accent in children and adults. *Modern Language Journal, 98*(1), 432–449. doi: 10.1111/j.1540-4781.2014.12059.x

Wagner, M., & Watson, D. G. (2010). Experimental and theoretical advances in prosody: A review. *Language and cognitive processes, 25*(7–9), 905–945. doi: 10.1080/01690961003589492

Walsh, S. (2013). *Classroom discourse and teacher development.* Edinburgh: Edinburgh University Press. doi: 10.3366/j.ctt1g0b484.6

Willis, J. (1992). Inner and outer: Spoken discourse in the language classroom. In M. Coulthard (Ed.), *Advances in spoken discourse analysis* (pp. 162–182). London: Routledge. doi: 10.4324/9780203200063

2 Directing attention

Introduction

Speech styles such as SDS are characterized by more formal, careful speech that involves clear articulatory cues produced through manipulations occurring at both the segmental and suprasegmental levels (Burnham, Gamache, Bergeson, & Dilley, 2013; Quilis, 1981). Speakers complement and manipulate linguistic information with paralinguistic information, i.e., vocal signals beyond the verbal level, which conveys their attitude, emotions, or speaking style through the prosodic parameters of duration, intensity, and pitch (Ephratt, 2011; Hirst, 2006; House, 2006; Yamashita, 2013). Duration accounts for articulation rate, intensity refers to the loudness of the voice, and pitch relates to how the frequency of sound waves, i.e., fundamental frequency (F0),[1] is perceived. All these prosodic correlates vary according to the individual, the speech setting and context, the interlocutors, the topic of conversation, etc.

In L2 classrooms, prosody can be quite complex due to the multiplicity of communicative and pragmatic functions of SDS. In addition to the paralinguistic functions that are carried out during everyday speech, L2 teachers utilize the prosodic tools at their disposal to engage learners, draw attention to target items, communicate the relative importance of speech segments, guide classroom discourse, and facilitate comprehension (Chaudron, 1988; Christie, 2002; Rao, 2006; Walsh, 2013). Other factors that likely also influence duration, intensity, and pitch in L2 classrooms include, but are not limited to, the teacher's personality, attitude and feelings, linguistic background, education and training, and professional experience. In order to begin the exploration of the subtle (and at times not so subtle) manipulations at the prosodic level that occur in the speech of L2 teachers, it is first important to understand the linguistic concepts involved in speech prominence, tease apart what we know about the relative influence of prosodic correlates on stress and focus, and shine a light on other factors that affect speech melody such as an individual's biology, departure from prosodic conventions, communication of information in the discourse, and pitch excursions at phrasal boundaries. It is necessary to outline the linguistic phenomena at the backbone of speech analysis at the suprasegmental level before entering the discussion of speech styles and contexts relevant to the exploration of SDS in L2 classrooms.

Prosodic prominence

Stress

Stress is defined as acoustic prominence placed on a word, sentence, or phrase relative to others in an utterance (Ortega-Llebaria & Prieto, 2007). *Word-level stress*, also called *lexical* or *primary stress*, is a contrastive feature of many languages including English, Italian, and Spanish (Chun, 2002; Ortega-Llebaria & Prieto, 2007). In Spanish, a particular syllable in a given stressed word is lexically specified to carry stress,[2] and displacing the stress could change the word's meaning (Beckman, Díaz-Campos, McGory, & Morgan, 2002). For example, the words *papa* 'potato' and *papá* 'dad' form a minimal pair who's only distinguishing feature is the placement of stress on the tonic syllable. Quilis (1981) enumerates a list of types of words that are stressed when used in isolation, and in theory, are accompanied by F0 movement.[3] These include nouns, adjectives, tonic pronouns, indefinite adjectives and pronouns, possessive pronouns, demonstratives, numbers, verbs, adverbs,[4] and interrogative question words.

While stressed words are typically accompanied by F0 movement, at the discourse-level, acoustic prominence may or may not correspond with words that are lexically specified for primary stress (Ortega-Llebaria & Prieto, 2007). In fact, in certain contexts, lexically unstressed words can receive stress (Hualde, 2009). For example, the question *¿fuiste al mercado por tu mamá?* 'did you go to the market for your mom?' could be answered in several ways, and the speaker places acoustic prominence on the syllable that communicates the desired response. Perhaps you did not go to the market for your mom, but instead went with your mom. You would then respond with a sentence like *no, fui al mercado con ella* 'no, I went to the market with her' placing acoustic prominence on the preposition *con* that contrasts with the preposition *por* from the original question. This observation is in support of the view of stress as a discourse-level phenomenon that is intimately associated with intonation. For the remainder of this book, the word *stress* is used to refer to acoustic prominence that may or may not cued by F0 movement and *accent* is used to refer to observed F0 movement through the stressed syllable.

Intonation

Phrase-level intonation, often defined as the melody of speech, is the manipulation of pitch in order to fulfill linguistic functions such as communicating discourse information and paralinguistic functions such as expressing pragmatic meaning (Ladd, 2008; O'Rourke, 2012b; Prieto, 2015; Yamashita, 2013). From a phonological perspective, pitch modulation throughout an utterance is independent from other phonological features and should be analyzed separately from segments, i.e., autosegmentally (Hualde, 2003). Pierrehumbert (1980) first developed the Autosegmental-Metrical (AM) framework of intonational phonology in her analysis of English with the goal of identifying the contrastive features of intonation, and the theory has since been applied to Spanish by Estebas Vilaplana and Prieto (2008), Face and Prieto (2007), Hualde (2003), Hualde and Prieto (2016), Nibert (2000), and Sosa (1999), among others. The model is considered *metrical* because the autosegmental tiers are made up of phrasal constituents that are organized hierarchically, with each tier coming together to form the higher tier (Gussenhoven, 2002b; Nibert, 2000; Rao, 2007, 2008, 2009). Syllables make up a foot that makes up a phonological word (PW). PWs constitute phonological phrases (PPHs), similar to intermediate phrases *(ips)*, which are a part of the larger intonational phrase (IP) in an utterance.

Inspired by the basic principles of the AM model, the Spanish transcription system called the Spanish Tones and Break Indices (Sp_ToBI) provides conventions that specify the F0 high (H) and low (L) tones (i.e., phonological targets or anchoring points with intervening phonetic-level F0 movement) throughout an utterance in order to identify the presence of phrase boundary tones, i.e., tones that garnish the edges of phrases, which help group words that informationally go together, or word-level pitch accents[5] associated with stressed syllables (Aguilar, de la Mota, & Prieto, 2009; Beckman et al., 2002; Hualde, 2002, 2003). A pitch accent is defined as "a local feature of a pitch contour – usually but not invariably a pitch change, and often involving a local maximum – which signals that the syllable with which it is associated is prominent in the utterance" (Ladd, 2008, p. 48).

The AM framework and Sp_ToBI labeling system are undoubtedly useful in providing a descriptive framework for the analysis of intonation; however, there has traditionally been a clear divide between phonological analysis associated with determining linguistic meaning and phonetic analysis, which focuses on variation and paralinguistic meaning (Ladd, 2008; Pierrehumbert, 1980; Prieto, 2015). While this volume refers to concepts related to the framework, analyses based in the AM model and Sp_ToBI labeling system are not central to this work given the highly gradient, variable nature of the naturally occurring, unscripted speech data. The present objectives are to describe the variability of prosodic behaviors used during SDS by referring to both acoustic data and qualitative information. Furthermore, speech used in L2 classrooms is deeply rooted in the interactions that occur within these social spaces where there are many functions of intonation, so intonational form does not always map cleanly onto perceived meaning; that is, the speaker's intentions may not be transparent through their pitch (Prieto, 2015). Therefore, adhering to the AM framework would be less useful as a means of fulfilling the goals of the present explorations[6] (Hall, 2015; van Oostendorp, 2013).

Focus

Variability in intonational contours is responsible for the portrayal of special emphasis (Couper-Kuhlen, 2015). *Narrow focus contexts* occur when one portion of an utterance is emphasized over another, while *broad focus contexts* occur when all the information in an utterance is highlighted equally (Face, 2006). Face (2006) explains that narrow focus includes both contexts in which new information is introduced and *contrastive focus contexts* where an element in an utterance is emphasized in order to draw attention to its divergence from the interlocutor's assumption. Referring back to the previous example about going to the *mercado* 'market', it was apparent in the initial question that the speaker believed you went to the market as a favor for your mother. In order to correct that assumption, you placed added prominence on the contrastive feature in your response, the preposition *con* in the sentence *no, fui al mercado con ella* 'no, I went to the market with her.' While recent research has shown that duration, intensity, and pitch play a role in marking relative prominence, pitch is believed to be the most important indicator followed by duration, and then intensity (Face, 2003, 2006; Olson & Ortega-Llebaria, 2010; O'Rourke, 2012b).

In broad focus contexts and at fast speech rates that are typical of casual or spontaneous speech, it is common that F0 peaks on non-focal words are suppressed (Face, 2003; Rao, 2006). Rao (2006) examined semi-spontaneous speech samples from Madrid Spanish and found that F0 movement was reduced when words were frequent, repeated, or communicatively unimportant to the task at hand. He also discovered that pitch suppression was very rare in utterances that were emotionally charged or emphasized. In a later study, Rao (2009) explored the phenomenon of F0 suppression in spontaneous speech in Barcelona and discovered that some words and linguistic conditions were more susceptible to reduction than others, showing that F0 peak suppression is common and systematic. However, this is not true of all Spanish speech communities (Rao & Sessarego, 2016; Sessarego & Rao, 2016). In a pair of recent studies on Afro-Bolivian Spanish (ABS), an Afro-Hispanic variety spoken in Los Yungas, Bolivia, Rao and Sessarego (2016) and Sessarego and Rao (2016) found extremely low frequencies of F0 suppression in spontaneous speech as if the speakers were placing emphasis rampantly throughout their utterances. This connection between emphasis and F0 peak frequency is relevant to our discussion of SDS where special emphasis contexts are likely.

In Spanish broad focus contexts, the most prominent syllable in a phrase is the last stressed syllable in phrase-final position. This is consistent with Chomsky and Halle's (1968) Nuclear Stress Rule (NSR) which hypothesizes that prominence is assigned to the rightmost constituent in a given domain (relative to the domain above it) of the prosodic hierarchy. Deviation from this stress pattern signals either contrast or special emphasis on a particular lexical item (Ladd, 2008). Although it is more common in Spanish to mark focus through word order (Zubizarreta, 1994), it is also possible to acoustically emphasize a pre-nuclear word to express narrow focus, contrastive focus, or informational (also known as presentational) focus (Hoot, 2012; Ladd, 2008). This special emphasis is achieved through an increase in pitch range and earlier peak alignment in words receiving narrow focus relative to broad-focused constituents[7] (Olson & Ortega-Llebaria, 2010).

The transfer of main stress to the focal constituent of an utterance is a phenomenon known as *stress shift* (Hoot, 2012). Hoot (2012) discovered that both heritage and monolingual speakers of Mexican Spanish use stress shift as a cue for presentational focus. He defines presentational focus as a type of narrow focus when emphasis is placed on the part of the utterance that is new or particularly important for the listener. These trends have also been observed in Peninsular varieties of Spanish. Face (2006) compared the realization of narrow focus in declarative and interrogative sentence types in Peninsular varieties of Spanish and found that narrow focus is marked in both sentence types by a higher F0 peak and leftward F0 peak movement. In narrow focus absolute interrogatives (i.e., yes–no questions), the focal word is also marked by boundary pitch movement (BPM) at the ends of phrases and sometimes a pause. However, the debate continues about which acoustic correlates are most salient when cuing stress (Hirst, 2006; Navarro Tomás, 1944; Ortega-Llebaria, 2006).

Because narrow focus and special emphasis contexts are pervasive in L2 classrooms, the prosodic realization of stress and focus during SDS is a key area of exploration. The following section goes into detail about the prosodic correlates of stress and focus that will guide data analyses in the present investigation.

Acoustic correlates of stress and focus

Duration

Relative length of constituents has traditionally been identified as one of the main correlates of stress. Although previous research has linked vowel length and syllable duration to the portrayal of accentuation and narrow focus marking (Gut, Trouvain, & Barry, 2007), the tokens extracted for acoustic analysis in the present investigation are phrasal units, so measuring for vowel and syllable length is logistically impractical. Instead, the measurement of duration that will prove to be most feasible and relevant to the research questions at hand is that of articulation rate,[8] which is calculated by dividing the number of syllables in a phrase by its duration in seconds.

Speech rate has substantial communicative and social implications, and thus is a vital component of L2 pedagogy. Swiftness of speech is commonly linked to the perception of fluency and general language proficiency (Gut et al., 2007). Cucchiarini, Strik, and Boves (2002) found that NSs tend to use speech rate to judge fluency, with a faster rate correlating with greater fluency. Because speech rate is so closely associated with fluency, one of the common objectives of the L2 classroom, it is of particular interest to observe how individual L2 teachers manipulate articulation rate during SDS. L2 teachers can increase their speech rate in order to challenge students' comprehension skills or to mimic more natural, vernacular speech in the TL. Nevertheless, rate of speech is also intimately tied to comprehension and special emphasis. L2 teachers may slow down their articulation rate to make themselves more comprehensible or emphasize that something is important. Gut et al. (2007) reported that segments of less communicative importance are often articulated at a faster speech rate compared to more important utterances that correlate with a slower speech rate, showing that it is plausible that reduced speech rate is a prosodic feature used to mark the relative importance of speech constituents during SDS. So, the question remains as to what extent L2 teachers manipulate articulation rate for pedagogical purposes at the expense of modeling authentic spontaneous speech and preparing students for real-world speech comprehension.

Speech rate is also particularly relevant to the investigation at hand because it is affected by speech style and context, and because it also influences pitch. In general, speakers use slower articulation rates during formal, monitored speech acts and faster articulation rates during informal, unmonitored speech, though there is variation according to individuals and the context of the speech act (Face, 2003). For instance, Cucchiarini et al.

(2002) found a lack of consistency in articulation rate during spontaneous speech when compared to the more constant rate of read speech. Speech rate also varies according to the communicative weight of the utterance regardless of speech modality (i.e., read versus spontaneous speech), as noted above. Additionally, variation in speech rate has consequences on the realization of pitch. In faster, less monitored speech that typically occurs during spontaneous speech styles, F0 contours tend to be suppressed. Speakers have less time to produce multiple F0 peaks, and, therefore, F0 peak suppression is more likely to occur (Rao, 2009).

Due to the fact that SDS and conversational speech both represent naturally-occurring, spontaneous speech but differ in terms of style and context, speech rate is expected to be a key factor that differentiates SDS from conversational speech.

Intensity

Traditionally, it was assumed that intensity was the main feature affecting prosodic prominence in stressed syllables (Navarro Tomás, 1944). Intensity, measured in decibels (dB), is the amplitude of a sound wave, which represents the amount of pressure expelled during articulation (Chun, 2002; Hirst, 2006). It is influenced by how loudly or softly the speaker is speaking, and the relative intensity of sounds can contribute to acoustic prominence. Nevertheless, in studies on stress and focus, the role of intensity has been inconsistent. Some researchers identified a correlation between stressed syllables and higher levels of intensity (Hualde, 2003; Navarro Tomás, 1964). In an experimental study on the interaction between intensity and accent, Toledo (1989) verified the important role of intensity. He found that intensity was the most consistent cue of prominence in Buenos Aires Spanish.

However, the importance of intensity as a cue to prominence has been refuted in many recent studies. Face (2000) found that intensity was not a significant factor in marking narrow focus in the Spanish of Madrid. Ortega-Llebaria (2006) also found inconsistent results with regards to the intensity patterns across the different speakers in her study representing both Peninsular and Latin American varieties of Spanish and concluded that intensity is an optional trigger to stress. In a later study, Ortega-Llebaria and Prieto (2011) examined how overall intensity interacts with stress and discovered only minimal intensity differences between stressed segments and adjacent unstressed segments in Spanish read speech. However, the authors claimed that this could have been an artifact of the sentence types employed in their study, as participants used intensity to mark stress more in reporting clauses, or indirect speech where speakers quote another person and attribute the quote to that person. In light of these disparate findings, it can be concluded that while overall intensity is likely not the main cue to marking prominence, it may be important, especially when considered in conjunction with other correlates of stress such as duration and pitch (Chun, 2002).

Therefore, while intensity has received relatively less attention in recent research on prosodic prominence, it is still important when looking at the big picture of marking stress and accent in Spanish (Hualde, 2005). Prominence marking is rampant in formal speech styles, so intensity is considered in this investigation in order to determine its strength as a feature that distinguishes SDS from other speech styles.

Fundamental frequency range, mean, and peak height

As a speaker's vocal cords vibrate, the frequency of the vibration determines the pitch of the utterance as perceived by the listener (Chun, 2002). This sound wave frequency is called F0 and is measured in hertz (Hz), or cycles per second (O'Rourke, 2012a). Faster vibrations sound like higher pitches to the ear of the listener, and slower vibrations sound like lower pitches (Hirst, 2006; Ohala, 1984). Pitch is the key prosodic correlate at play in the marking of special emphasis and narrow focus (Face, 2007; Olson & Ortega-Llebaria, 2010). Speakers have the ability to manipulate their average pitch overall, their pitch range, and the height of F0 peaks in order to emphasize a segment of speech, and a shift in F0 mean and range marks a change in pitch register. It is common for speakers to use the lower third of their vocal range in broad focused intonational contours (Cruttenden, 1997). A sudden switch to a considerably higher or lower pitch (within articulatory limits) is considered marked, or intended to portray special meaning, and is used to mark discourse transitions (Riou, 2017). This register shift has also been observed during direct reported speech (Alvord, 2010b; Face, 2011; Jansen, Gregory, & Brenier, 2001; Klewitz & Couper-Kuhlen, 1999).

In narrow focus and special emphasis contexts, focal accents are typically produced with a high F0 peak and are accompanied by utterance-medial F0 suppression, although this phenomenon is not systematic (Beckman et al., 2002; Hualde, 2007; O'Rourke, 2012b). Hualde (2007) reported data showing that stressed phrase-medial words in exclamatives were not accompanied by F0 movement, probably due to the increase in relative salience of the focal item. However, O'Rourke (2012b) compared F0 peak height in contrastive focus segments produced by speakers from Lima and Cuzco, Peru, and discovered that while speakers from Cuzco used reduced F0 peaks in syllables following the focal syllable to mark contrastive focus, speakers from Lima employed a higher F0 peak height. Because the suppression of F0 peaks in Spanish is not categorical and is employed differently in different dialects and across different speech styles and contexts, F0 mean alone does not necessarily represent the full picture of prosodic prominence.

Consider, for instance, the declarative intonational contour displayed in Figure 2.1, which comes from O'Rourke's (2012b) corpus of speech samples from the Lima speakers. The sentence "*su familia mandará los violines*" 'his family will send the violins' is shown in broad focus in (a) and again in contrastive focus in (b) with the focus on the subject, *familia* 'family.' The broad focus utterance contains F0 rises associated with stressed syllables, a gradual decay of F0 peaks throughout the phrase (i.e., *downstepping*), and late F0 peak alignment in pre-tonic syllables. On the other hand, the contrastive focus utterance has an F0 peak associated with the focal item and suppression of post-focal peaks. The highest F0 peak in (b) reaches a greater F0 value than in (a), but due to the presence of post-focal F0 excursions in the broad focus utterance and the suppression of that movement during contrastive focus, the mean F0 value of both utterances is approximately 130 Hz. However, if we subtract the value of the lowest valley from the value of the highest peak in a phrase, the noteworthy intonational differences between the two utterances become more evident. The F0 range in (a) is approximately 102 Hz while the F0 range in (b) is approximately 125 Hz.

The difference in pitch range between broad and narrow focus contexts is not unique to Peruvian varieties of Spanish. In fact, pitch range is systematically narrower during neutral, broad focus speech contexts (Olson & Ortega-Llebaria, 2010; Rao, 2006; Warren, 2016). In Olson and Ortega-Llebaria's

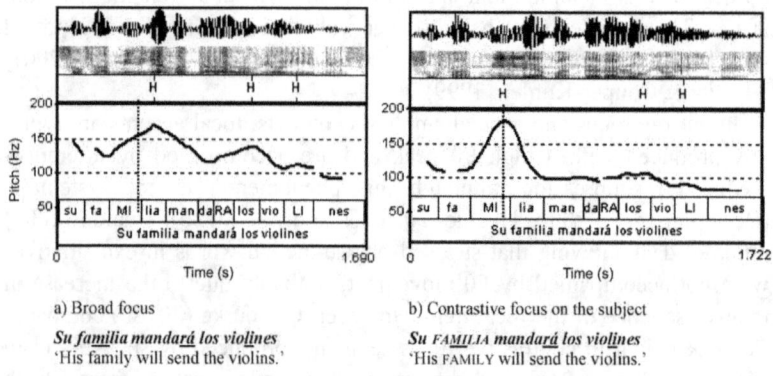

a) Broad focus

Su familia mandará los violines
'His family will send the violins.'

b) Contrastive focus on the subject

Su FAMILIA mandará los violines
'His FAMILY will send the violins.'

Figure 2.1 Broad focus versus contrastive focus intonation.

(2010) perceptual study on the identification of narrow focus, participants heard stimuli that varied in pitch range, with some utterances exhibiting only minimal differences between F0 valleys and F0 peaks and others with relatively more extreme changes in pitch. A wider pitch range used in the stimuli was positively correlated with identification of narrow focus contexts.

Consistent with the behavior of speakers from Lima in O'Rourke's (2012b) study, other research has highlighted the importance of F0 peak height in marking special emphasis (de la Mota, 1997; Face, 2001, 2007, 2011; Toledo, 1989). De la Mota (1997) found that F0 peaks associated with contrastive focus items were higher than those of broad focus constituents. Face (2007) claimed that in both declarative and interrogative speech types it is actually F0 peak height that is the crucial factor in marking narrow focus as opposed to pitch range. The most common strategy speakers used was a higher F0 peak associated with the focal word in the utterance.

Because of the observed influences of F0 mean, range, and peak height in marking discourse cues, special meaning, and narrow focus, these correlates are considered as potential features distinguishing SDS from other speech types.

Speech melody

Pitch register

Pitch varies according to age and gender. The size of articulatory organs correlates with the speed at which vocal cords vibrate, and thus, perceived pitch (Gussenhoven, 2002a). Consequently, a speaker's pitch is perceived as higher when they are in the beginning stages of life and their larynx and vocal cords are still growing. Vocal anatomy is similar for all sexes in these early stages of development; then around the age of puberty, their development diverges, causing adult males to have a 50% larger larynx in the anterior-posterior dimension when compared to females (Gussenhoven, 2002a; Ohala, 1984). As a result, male vocal cords are longer and lower in the throat than females' and, thus, vibrate at a slower rate and allow males to speak with a lower pitch. Adult male speakers produce F0 ranges that vary between 60 Hz and 240 Hz on average, while the average range for adult female speakers is between 180 Hz and 400 Hz (Chun, 2002). Of course, these averages are generalizations based on an imagined gender dichotomy, and certainly there are individuals across the spectrum with regard to pitch range.

Speakers also manipulate pitch according to style and context in order to fulfill informational or communicative purposes. Gussenhoven (2002a) theorizes about biological codes that relate to pitch production and perception, and Hirschberg (2002) discusses how the adherence to or violation of these codes relates to conversational conventions (i.e., maxims). Largely based on the proposals of Ohala (1984), Gussenhoven names three biological codes that are universally responsible for variation: the frequency code, the effort code, and the production code. The frequency code refers to pitch variation due to the anatomical differences between children, adult women, and adult men, and is commonly associated with the portrayal of affect, i.e., attitude and emotion. A high pitch register corresponds with "friendliness, politeness, vulnerability or protectiveness," while lower pitches bring about feelings of "aggression or scathingness" (Warren, 2016, p. 17). Because it is linked to the rate of vibration of the vocal cords, a high pitch register can also indicate more involvement on behalf of the speaker, such as when they are in a position of authority. The frequency code is also responsible for portraying certainty (L tones) and uncertainty (H tones). The effort code relates to the amount of energy that is expended during speech production, which is realized as pitch range. Speakers widen their pitch range to express surprise, content, and kindness, as can be seen in child-directed speech (CDS), or in some cases to express special emphasis or salience (Gussenhoven, 2002a; Rao, 2006; Warren, 2016). Finally, the production code denotes the amount of effort expended at different points during a given utterance. Information is portrayed through the production code to mark either communicative relevance (e.g., a H tone in the beginning of an utterance corresponds with new information and a L tone corresponds with old information) or discourse cues (e.g., phrase-final rises indicate that the speaker is not yet finished with their talk turn, and terminal falls indicate finality).

Although these biological codes correspond with communicative conventions in speech production, a violation of these communicative conventions, many of which are language-specific, conveys a message in and of itself. Hirschberg (2002) gives the example of the rising contour associated with absolute interrogatives and uncertainty in many languages, including most dialects of English and Spanish. She explains that speakers have the ability to "exploit the shared knowledge of the maxim to different effect, e.g., by using a rising contour to convey irony or to produce a rhetorical question" (p. 67).

Given the documented anatomical differences between speakers according to gender and age, it is important to control for these variables when selecting participants for experimental studies on speech prosody. Additionally, Gussenhoven's (2002a) and Hirschberg's (2002) biological codes and maxims describe many of the speech functions that are likely pervasive in the L2 classroom, such as the expression of affect, special emphasis, communicative importance, and discourse cues; therefore, these codes and maxims are referenced in the interpretations of prosodic correlates measured in the present analyses.

Variation in declarative intonation

Analyses of intonational contours have revealed that both discourse information as well as illocutionary information and pragmatic cues are portrayed through the intonational contour patterns (Chun, 2002; Couper-Kuhlen, 2015; Hualde, 2003; Ladd, 1996). F0 movement is the main prosodic feature that distinguishes a declarative from an interrogative utterance in Spanish (Face, 2007). In fact, in many dialects of Spanish, F0 movement can be the sole cue to utterance type in isomorphic utterances (Alvord, 2010a, 2010b; Willis, 2005). As an example, out of context, the sentence *ya llegó el autobús* 'the bus already arrived' is only distinguished from its interrogative counterpart *¿ya llegó el autobús?* 'the bus already arrived?' through the intonational pattern employed by the speaker. In Spanish, there are common intonational contours that correspond with utterance type.

Neutral, broad focus declaratives are characterized by an F0 peak associated with each stressed syllable throughout the IP (Face, 2003). Common traits of broad focus declaratives observed in both Peninsular and Latin American dialects of Spanish include downstepping of non-final F0 peaks throughout the intonational contour, late F0 peak alignment in non-final F0 peaks, and final F0 peak alignment accompanied by falling BPM (Beckman et al., 2002; Estebas Vilaplana, & Prieto, 2008; Face, 2002; Hualde, 2003; Prieto & Roseano, 2010; Prieto, Shih, & Nibert, 1996; Sosa, 1999; Willis, 2005). An example of a broad focus declarative utterance that follows these trends is presented in Figure 2.2. The speech sample comes from the conversational speech data reported in this book. In this figure showing the intonational contour of the phrase "*han visto El laberinto del fauno*" 'they have seen *Pan's Labyrinth*,' the black arrows point to accented syllables, in this case "*visto*" 'seen,' "*laberinto*" 'labyrinth,' and "*fauno*" 'fawn.' There is an F0 peak associated with each of the stressed words throughout the phrase, and each non-initial peak is downstepped relative to the previous peak. Additionally, F0 peaks associated with pre-nuclear stressed syllables are realized post-tonically, or immediately following the stressed syllable, while the nuclear accent is aligned within the confines of the final stressed syllable.

Despite the relative consistency of pre-nuclear peak patterns in declarative utterances in laboratory speech data, there is considerable variation across speech styles and regional dialects (Face, 2001; Hualde, 2003;

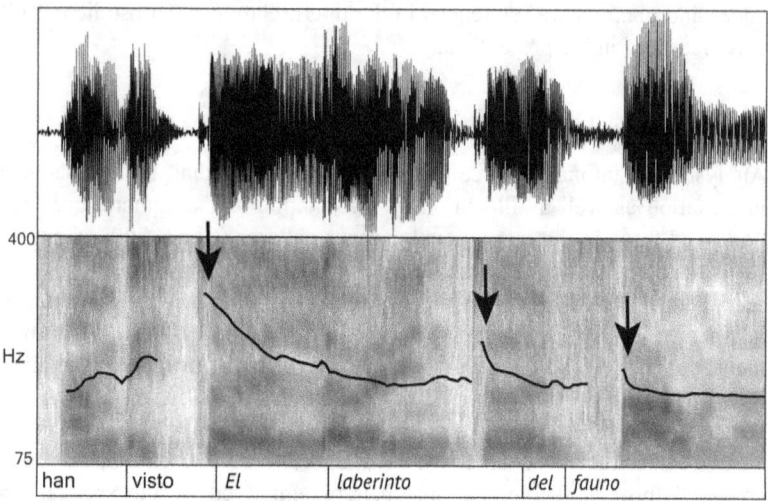

Figure 2.2 Broad focus declarative intonation.

O'Rourke, 2006). For instance, several researchers have shown an upstepped pre-nuclear peak pattern in declaratives (Hualde, 2002; Nibert, 2000). *Upstepping* is defined as "a tonal event that occurs higher than preceding events" (O'Rourke, 2006, p. 62). Hualde (2002) reported upstep in Castilian Spanish declaratives, and O'Rourke (2006) found upstepping as a feature of read speech for Spanish speakers from both Lima and Cuzco, Peru. The functions of upstepping are not systematic across dialects and styles, so it is likely that upstep is used to fulfill a number of different communicative and pragmatic functions such as partitioning a sentence and marking contrastive focus (Hualde, 2002, 2003; Nibert, 2000). Furthermore, upstepping is believed to be related to marking phrase edges, as high-rising BPM triggers raising of non-final F0 peaks (Nibert, 2000).

In addition to variation in the shape of utterance-medial pitch contours, there is considerable variation in pitch at phrasal boundaries. Final rising boundary tones are typically a feature of absolute interrogatives (Face, 2006), but in Cuban Spanish spoken in Miami, for instance, researchers have reported final falling pitch contours in absolute interrogatives resembling broad focus declaratives (Alvord, 2010b). This lack of consistency in shape of utterance-final pitch movement across Spanish dialects brings about other questions as to the relative strength of prosodic cues. Face (2011) investigated to what degree different constituents of the intonational contour cue listeners to sentence type. Castilian Spanish stimuli exhibited common intonational contours that differentiate declaratives from interrogatives, and participants were asked to identify the sentence type and the naturalness of the utterances at different moments. The results showed that listeners are 100% accurate in identifying sentence type prior to final BPM, but that the final cue is the most powerful and can override previous cues. He concluded that because there are many redundant cues for sentence type, the individual cues themselves do not carry very much communicative burden.

The data used for the present analyses was limited to declarative utterances in order to eliminate the possibility of contour shape being attributable to sentence type. In addition, the evidence that sentence type is communicated prior to the utterance-final cue is relevant because, without being charged with the communicative weight it was once thought to carry, phrase boundaries are free to serve other functions such as portraying pragmatic meaning and discourse information, functions that are likely prevalent in SDS.

Phrase boundaries

Pitch movement at phrase boundaries is particularly crucial in communicating pragmatic meaning. Phrase boundaries typically consist of falling or rising tones that indicate the beginning or end of an IP and are usually accompanied by pre-boundary syllable and vowel lengthening and followed by a clear, long pause signaling the end of an idea (Estebas Vilaplana & Prieto, 2008; Prieto, 2006; Rao, 2007, 2008, 2010; Sosa, 1999). However, it is possible for prosodic cues at phrase boundaries to be implemented by speakers differentially to fulfill communicative and pragmatic goals. Prieto and Roseano (2010) showed the relative power of the nuclear position in communicating discourse information and pragmatic messages across 10 dialectal varieties of Spanish. Final pitch movement was reported as a tactic for portraying emphasis, politeness, exclamation, and other "special pragmatic readings" (p. 290). Rao (2010) analyzed read speech by speakers of Spanish from Cuba, Ecuador, and Spain and found that while speakers exhibited final lengthening at both PPH and IP junctures, lengthening was associated with shorter pauses. The author concluded that prosodic cues do not necessarily operate in conjunction to signal a phrase boundary and cues "provide different pragmatic and communicative functions" (Rao, 2010, p. 79). In sum, each prosodic cue to phrase boundary is a tool in the speaker's style toolbox.

High-rising boundary tones in particular have been linked to the portrayal of pragmatic meaning and discourse information. For instance, *uptalk* (also known as *upspeak* or *high-rising terminal* (HRT)) has been described as having a confirmation-seeking function that is used often during narrative-style speech or instruction-giving to command the listeners' attention or check for understanding (Fletcher, Stirling, Mushin, & Wales, 2002; Ladd, 1996; Warren, 2005, 2016). Ladd (1996) describes the intonational pattern as a high-rising boundary tone that serves as "a kind of shorthand for 'Do you follow me?'" (p. 121). Warren (2016) provides a more precise definition of uptalk as "a marked rising intonation pattern found at the end of intonation units realized on declarative utterances, and which serves primarily to check comprehension or to seek feedback" (p. 2). The rises are markedly different than other expected intonational rises and are not intended to ask a question.

Uptalk has been reported as a feature of spontaneous speech in several dialects of English including British English (Bradford, 1997; Cruttenden, 2007), New Zealand English (Warren, 2005, 2016), Australian English (Guy & Vonwiller, 1989; Inoue, 2006), and American English dialects (Podesva, 2011; Ritchart & Arvaniti, 2014). In addition to the communicative functions mentioned above, HRT has been reported as a signal of continuity or non-finality (House, 2006), and is used to convey irony and pose rhetorical questions (Hirschberg, 2002). Final high-rising intonation is also commonly attributed to affective meanings such as politeness, sensitivity, compassion, and friendliness (Bradford, 1997; House, 2006; Podesva, 2011). Bradford (1997) explains that the HRT can act as "a bonding technique to promote a sense of solidarity and empathy between speakers and hearers" (p. 34).

Although uptalk has not been reported nearly as much in Spanish as it has in English, impressionistic accounts of both Mexican and Dominican dialects do describe HRT intonation similar to that of English uptalk (Prieto & Roseano, 2010). One of the few experimental studies that explores the use of uptalk in Spanish dialects is Vergara's (2015) investigation of the speech used by contestants of a televised Spanish dating show. Vergara confirms the existence of uptalk in Spanish used by both the male and female participants in his study, and projects that the functions of uptalk include "holding the floor" during a talk turn, providing emotional comfort, being sensitive, and flirting (pp. 193–194). The functions listed by Vergara align with those found in other studies on English uptalk.

Due to relative communicative strength of the nuclear position in Spanish, phrasal segmentation and boundary marking are relevant in the examination of SDS prosody (Chomsky & Halle, 1968; Prieto & Roseano, 2010).

Notes

1 The terms pitch and F0 are used interchangeably throughout this book to refer to the frequency of sound waves.
2 Adverbs ending in –*mente* have two stressed syllables, the stressed syllable of the root word and the stressed syllable *men* in the suffix –*mente* (Quilis, 1981).
3 Quilis cautions that many times lexical stress associated with a word is subject to movement, removal, or addition when it is used during connected discourse (Quilis, 1981, pp. 390–391).
4 Adverbs can be stressed or unstressed depending on their function (Quilis, 1981, p. 395).
5 Intonational pitch accents are not to be confused with lexically specified pitch accents that are contrastive features of tone languages such as many Eastern Asian and some European languages (Hualde, 2003; Ladd, 2008). In intonation languages such as English and Spanish, pitch accents express meaning at the sentence-level as well as pragmatic meaning (O'Rourke, 2012a).
6 More information about the AM theory as it applies to Spanish intonation is available through Aguilar et al. (2009) and Beckman et al. (2002).
7 It is common to find F0 peaks in pre-nuclear position realized within the tonic syllable in special emphasis and narrow focus contexts. In neutral, broad focus contexts, F0 peaks prior to the final peak in a phrase are typically realized just after the tonic syllable, while the final peak in the phrase aligns within the bounds of the tonic syllable (Olson & Ortega-Llebaria, 2010; O'Rourke, 2012b).
8 The terms articulation rate and speech rate are used interchangeably to refer to the same feature.

References

Aguilar, L., de la Mota, C., & Prieto, P. (Eds.). (2009). *Sp_ToBI training materials*. Retrieved from http://prosodia.upf.edu/sp_tobi/en/index.php

Alvord, S. M. (2010a). Miami Cuban Spanish declarative intonation. *Studies in Hispanic and Lusophone Linguistics, 3*(1), 3–39. doi: 10.1515/shll-2010-1064

Alvord, S. M. (2010b). Variation in Miami Cuban Spanish interrogative intonation. *Hispania, 93*(2), 235–255. doi: 10.1353/hpn.0.0052

Beckman, M. E., Díaz-Campos, M., McGory, J. T., & Morgan, T. A. (2002). Intonation across Spanish, in the Tones and Break Indices framework. *Probus, 14*(1), 9–36. doi: 10.1515/prbs.2002.008

Bradford, B. (1997). Upspeak in British English. *English Today, 13*(3), 29–36. doi: 10.1017/S0266078400009810

Burnham, E., Gamache, J. L., Bergeson, T., & Dilley, L. (2013). Voice-onset time in infant-directed speech over the first year and a half. *Proceedings of Meetings on Acoustics ICA2013, Montreal, 19*, 060094. doi: 10.1121/1.4800072

Chaudron, C. (1988). Teacher talk in second-language classrooms. In C. Chaudron (Ed.), *Second language classrooms* (pp. 50–89). Cambridge: Cambridge University Press. doi: 10.1017/CBO9781139524469.005

Chomsky, N., & Halle, M. (1968). *The sound pattern of English*. New York: Harper & Row.

Christie, F. (2002). Classroom discourse analysis: A functional perspective. *Bloomsbury Publishing*. doi: 10.1590/S0102-44502006000100012

Chun, D. M. (2002). *Discourse intonation in L2: From theory and research to practice*. Philadelphia, PA: John Benjamins. doi: 10.1075/lllt.1

Couper-Kuhlen, E. (2015). Intonation and discourse. In D. Tannen, H. Hamilton, & D. Schiffrin, *The handbook of discourse analysis* (2 ed., pp. 82–104). Hoboken, NJ: Wiley-Blackwell. doi: 10.1002/9781118584194.ch4

Cruttenden, A. (1997). *Intonation* (2 ed.). Cambridge: Cambridge University Press. doi: 10.1017/CBO9781139166973

Cruttenden, A. (2007). Intonational diglossia: A case study of Glasgow. *Journal of the International Phonetic Association, 37*(2), 257–274. doi: 10.1017/S0025100 307002915

Cucchiarini, C., Strik, H., & Boves, L. (2002). Quantitative assessment of second language learners fluency: Comparisons between read and spontaneous speech. *Acoustical Society of America, 111*(6). doi: 10.1121/1.1471894

de la Mota, C. (1997). Prosody of sentences with contrastive/new information in Spanish. In A. Botinis, G. Kouroupetroglou, & G. Carayiannis (Ed.), *Intonation: Theory, models and applications. Proceedings of an ESCA Workshop* (pp. 75–78). Athens, Greece.

Ephratt, M. (2011). Linguistic, paralinguistic and extralinguistic speech and silence. *Journal of Pragmatics, 43*, 2286–2307. doi: 10.1016/j.pragma.2011.03.006

Estebas Vilaplana, E., & Prieto, P. (2008). La notación prosódica en español. Une revisión del Sp_ToBI. *Estudios de Fonética Experimental, 17*, 263–283.

Face, T. L. (2000). Prosodic manifestations of focus in Spanish. *Southwest Journal of Linguistics, 19*(1), 45–62.

Face, T. L. (2001). *Intonational marking of contrastive focus in Madrid Spanish*, Ph. D. Dissertation. The Ohio State University.

Face. T. L. (2002). Local intonational marking of Spanish contrastive focus. *Probus, 14*(1), 71–92. doi: 10.1515/prbs.2002.006

Face, T. L. (2003). Intonation in Spanish declaratives: Difference between lab speech and spontaneous speech. *Catalan Journal of Linguistics*, 115–131. Retrieved from https://revistes.uab.cat/catJL

Face, T. L. (2006). Narrow focus intonation in Castilian Spanish absolute interrogatives. *Journal of Language and Linguistics, 5*(2), 295–311.

Face, T. L. (2007). The role of intonational cues in the perception of declaratives and absolute interrogatives in Castilian Spanish. *EFE, 16*, 185–225.

Face, T. L. (2011). *Perception of Castilian Spanish intonation: Implications for intonational phonology*. Munich: Lincom Europa.

Face, T., & Prieto, P. (2007). Rising Accents in Castilian Spanish: a revision of Sp-ToBI. *Journal of Portuguese Linguistics, 6*(1), 117–146. doi: 10.5334/jpl.147

Fletcher, J., Stirling, L., Mushin, I., & Wales, R. (2002). Intonational rises and dialog acts in the Australian English map task. *Language and Speech, 45*(3), 229–253. doi: 10.1177/00238309020450030201

Gussenhoven, C. (2002a). Intonation and interpretation: Phonetics and phonology. *Phonetics and phonology. In Speech Prosody 2002, International Conference*. Retrieved from https://perso.limsi.fr/mareuil/control/gussenhoven.pdf

Gussenhoven, C. (2002b). Phonology of intonation. State-of-the-article. *Glot International,* 6(9/10), 271–284. Retrieved from http://gep.ruhosting.nl/carlos/glotgussenhoven.pdf

Gut, U., Trouvain, J., & Barry, W. J. (2007). Bridging research on phonetic descriptions with knowledge from teaching practice: The case of prosody in non-native speech. In J. Trouvain, & U. Gut (Eds.), *Non-native prosody, phonetic description and teaching practice* (pp. 3–25). Berlin: Mouton de Gruyter. doi: 10.1515/9783110198751.0.3

Guy, G., & Vonwiller, J. (1989). The high rising tone in Australian English. In P. Collins, & D. Blair (Eds.), *Australian English: The language of a new society* (pp. 21–34). Queensland: University of Queensland Press.

Hall, K. C. (2015). Categorical segments, probabilistic models. In E. Raimy, & C. E. Cairns (Eds.), *The segment in phonetics and phonology* (pp. 129–148). Hoboken, NJ: Wiley-Blackwell. doi: 10.1002/9781118555491.ch6

Hirschberg, J. (2002). The pragmatics of intonational meaning. *In Speech Prosody 2002, International Conference.*

Hirst, D. J. (2006). Prosodic aspects of speech and language. In K. Brown, A. H. Anderson, M. Berns, G. Hirst, & J. Miller (Eds.), *Encyclopedia of language and linguistics* (2 ed., Vol. 10, pp. 167–178). Amsterdam and London: Elsevier. doi: 10.1016/B0-08-044854-2/00019-5

Hoot, B. (2012). *Presentational focus in heritage and monolingual Spanish* (Doctoral dissertation). Retrieved from ProQuest Dissertations and Theses database. (UMI No. 3551884)

House, J. (2006). Constructing a context with intonation. *Journal of Pragmatics, 38,* 1542–1558. doi: 10.1016/j.pragma.2005.07.005

Hualde, J. I. (2002). Intonation in Spanish and the other Ibero-Romance languages: Overview and status quaestionis. In C. Wiltshire, & J. Camps (Eds.), *Romance philology and variation* (pp. 101–115). Philadelphia, PA: John Benjamins. doi: 10.1075/cilt.217.10hua

Hualde, J. I. (2003). El modelo métrico y autosegmental. In P. Prieto (Ed.), *Teorías de la entonación.* Barcelona: Ariel.

Hualde, J. I. (2005). *The sounds of Spanish.* Cambridge: Cambridge University Press. doi: 10.1017/CBO9780511719943

Hualde, J. I. (2007). Stress removal and stress addition in Spanish. *Journal of Portuguese Linguistics,* 59–89. doi: 10.5334/jpl.145

Hualde, J. I. (2009). Unstressed words in Spanish. *Language Sciences, 31*(2–3), 199–212. doi: 10.1016/j.langsci.2008.12.003

Hualde, J. I., & Prieto, P. (2016). Towards an International Prosodic Alphabet (IPrA). *Laboratory Phonology: Journal of the Association for Laboratory Phonology, 7*(1), 5. doi: 10.5334/labphon.11

Inoue, F. (2006). Sociolinguistic characteristics of intonation. In Y. Kawaguchi, I. Fónagy, & T. Moriguchi (Eds.), *Prosody and syntax: Cross-linguistic perspectives* (pp. 197–223). Philadelphia, PA: John Benjamins. doi: 10.1075/ubli.3.12ino

Jansen, W., Gregory, M. L., & Brenier, J. M. (2001). Prosodic correlates of directly reported speech: Evidence from conversational speech. *Prosody in Speech*

Recognition and Understanding. Retrieved from www.isca-speech.org/archive_open/prosody_2001/
Klewitz, G., & Couper-Kuhlen, E. (1999). Quote-unquote: the role of prosody in the contextualization of reported speech sequences. *Pragmatics, 9*(4), 459–485. doi: 10.1075/prag.9.4.03kle
Ladd, R. D. (1996). *Intonational phonology.* Cambridge: Cambridge University Press.
Ladd, R. D. (2008). *Intonational phonology* (2 ed.). Cambridge: Cambridge University Press. doi: 10.1017/CBO9780511808814
Navarro Tomás, T. (1944). *Manual de entonación española.* New York, NY: Hispanic Institute in the United States.
Navarro Tomás, T. (1964). La medida de intensidad. *Boletín de Filología,* (16), 231–235.
Nibert, H. J. (2000). *Phonetic and phonological evidence for intermediate phrasing in Spanish Intonation.* (Unpublished doctoral dissertation). University of Illinois at Urbana-Champaign, Illinois.
Ohala, J. J. (1984). An ethological perspective on common cross-language utilization of F0 of voice. *Phonetica, 41,* 1–16. doi: 10.1159/000261706
Olson, D., & Ortega-Llebaria, M. (2010). The perceptual relevance of code switching and intonation in creating narrow focus. In M. Ortega-Llebaria (Ed.), *Selected Proceedings of the 4th Conference on Laboratory Approaches to Spanish Phonology* (pp. 57–68). Somerville, MA: Cascadilla Proceedings Project.
O'Rourke, E. (2006). The direction of inflection: Downtrends and uptrends in Peruvian Spanish broad focus declaratives. In M. Díaz-Campos (Ed.), *Selected Proceedings of the 2nd Conference on Laboratory Approaches to Spanish Phonetics and Phonology* (pp. 62–74). Somerville, MA: Cascadilla Proceedings Project.
O'Rourke, E. (2012a). Intonation in Spanish. In J. I. Hualde, A. Olarrea, & E. O'Rourke (Eds.), *Handbook of Hispanic linguistics* (pp. 173–191). Oxford: Wiley-Blackwell. doi: 10.1002/9781118228098.ch9
O'Rourke, E. (2012b). The realization of contrastive focus in Peruvian Spanish intonation. *Lingua,* 494–510. doi: 10.1016/j.lingua.2011.10.002
Ortega-Llebaria, M. (2006). Phonetic cues to stress and accent in Spanish. In M. Díaz-Campos (Ed.), *Selected Proceedings of the 2nd Conference on Laboratory Approaches to Spanish Phonetics and Phonology* (pp. 104–118). Somerville, MA: Cascadilla Proceedings Project.
Ortega-Llebaria, M., & Prieto, P. (2007). Disentangling stress from accent in Spanish: Production patterns of the stress contrast in deaccented syllables. In P. Prieto, J. Mascaró, & M. J. Solé (Eds.), *Segmental and prosodic issues in Romance phonology* (pp. 155–175). Philadelphia, PA: John Benjamins. doi: 10.1075/cilt.282.11ort
Ortega-Llebaria, M., & Prieto, P. (2011). Acoustic correlates of stress in Central Catalan and Castilian Spanish. *Language and Speech, 54*(1), 73–97. doi: 10.1177/0023830910388014
Pierrehumbert, J. (1980). *The phonology and phonetics of English intonation* (Doctoral dissertation). Retrieved from Massachusetts Institute of Technology. (1721.1/16065)

Podesva, R. J. (2011). Salience and the social meaning of declarative contours: Three case studies of gay professionals. *Journal of English Linguistics, 39*(3), 233–264. doi: 10.1177/0075424211405161

Prieto, P. (2006). Phonological phrasing in Spanish. In S. Colina, & F. Martínez (Eds.), *Optimality-theoretic advances in Spanish phonology* (pp. 39–60). Amsterdam/Philadelphia: John Benjamins. doi: 10.1075/la.99.03pri

Prieto, P. (2015). Intonational meaning. *Wiley Interdisciplinary Reviews: Cognitive Science, 6*(4), 371–381. doi: 10.1002/wcs.1352

Prieto, P., & Roseano, P. (Eds.). (2010). *Transcription of intonation of the Spanish language*. Muenchen: Lincom Europa. Retrieved from http://prosodia.upf.edu/home/arxiu/publicacions/prieto/transcription_intonation_spanish.php

Prieto, P., Shih, C., & Nibert, H. (1996). Pitch downtrend in Spanish. *Journal of Phonetics, 24*, 445–473. doi: 10.1006/jpho.1996.0024

Quilis, A. (1981). *Fonética acústica de la lengua expañola*. Madrid: Gredos.

Rao, R. (2006). On intonation's relationship with pragmatic meaning in Spanish. *Proceedings of the 8th Hispanic Linguistics Symposium* (pp. 103–115). Somerville, MA: Cascadilla Press.

Rao, R. (2007). On the phonological phrasing patterns in the Spanish of Lima, Perú. *Southwest Journal of Linguistics, 26*(1).

Rao, R. (2008). Observations on the roles of prosody and syntax in the phonological phrasing of Barcelona Spanish. *The Linguistics Journal, 3*(3), 85–131. Retrieved from www.linguistics-journal.com/

Rao, R. (2009). Deaccenting in spontaneous speech in Barcelona Spanish. *Studies in Hispanic and Lusophone Linguistics, 2*(1), 31–75. doi: 10.1515/shll-2009-1035

Rao, R. (2010). Final lengthening and pause duration in three dialects of Spanish. In M. Ortega-Llebaria (Ed.), *Selected Proceedings of the 4th Conference on Laboratory Approaches to Spanish Phonology* (pp. 69–82). Somerville, MA: Cascadilla Proceedings Project.

Rao, R., & Sessarego, S. (2016). On the intonation of Afro-Bolivian Spanish declaratives: Implications for a theory of Afro-Hispanic creole genesis. *Lingua, 174*, 45–64. doi: 10.1016/j.lingua.2015.12.006

Riou, M. (2017). The prosody of topic transition in interaction: Pitch register variations. *Language and Speech*, 1–21. doi: 10.1177/0023830917696337

Ritchart, A., & Arvaniti, A. (2014). The form and use of uptalk in Southern Californian English. *Proceedings of Meetings on Acoustics, 20*.

Sessarego, S., & Rao, R. (2016). On the simplification of a prosodic inventory: The Afro-Bolivian Spanish case. In A. Cuza, L. Czerwionka, & D. Olson (Eds.), *Inquires in Hispanic Linguistics* (pp. 171–190). doi: 10.1075/ihll.12

Sosa, J. M. (1999). *La entonación del español. Su estructura fónica, variabilidad y dialectología*. Madrid: Cátedra.

Toledo, G. A. (1989). Señales prosódicas del foco. *Revista Argentina de Lingüística, 5*(1–2), 205–230.

van Oostendorp, M. (2013). Phonology between theory and data. In S. R. Anderson, J. Moeschler, & F. Reboul (Eds.), *The language-cognition interface* (pp. 289–306). Geneva: Librairie Droz.

Vergara, D. (2015). Uptalk in Spanish dating shows? *University of Pennsylvania Working Papers in Linguistics, 21*(2). Retrieved from https://repository.upenn.edu/pwpl/vol.21/iss2/21

Walsh, S. (2013). *Classroom discourse and teacher development.* Edinburgh: Edinburgh University Press. doi: 10.3366/j.ctt1g0b484.6

Warren, P. (2005). Patterns of late rising in New Zealand English: Intonational variation or intonational change? *Language Variation and Change, 17*, 209–230. doi: 10.1017/S095439450505009X

Warren, P. (2016). *Uptalk: The phenomenon of rising intonation.* Cambridge: Cambridge University Press. doi: 10.1017/CBO9781316403570

Willis, E. W. (2005). Tonal Levels in Puebla Mexico Spanish Declaratives and Absolute Interrogatives. In R. S. Gess, E. J. Rubin, & K. Arregi (Eds.). Philadelphia, PA: John Benjamins. doi: 10.1075/cilt.272.21wil

Yamashita, Y. (2013). A review of paralinguistic information processing for natural speech communication. *Acoustical Science and Technology, 34*(2), 73–79. doi: 10.1250/ast.34.73

Zubizarreta, M. L. (1994). The grammatical representation of topic and focus: Implications for the structure of the clause. *Working Papers in Linguistics, 4*(1). Retrieved from http://hdl.handle.net/11707/457

3 Didactic speech accommodation and modification

Introduction

At some point in time, you may have noticed yourself speaking differently based on who you were addressing. You probably speak differently with your colleagues than with your boss, and you probably alter your speech when addressing children versus adults. Context greatly influences speech production. For example, consider how a weather reporter speaks when delivering the following forecast on national television: "It's hot and humid out today and tomorrow, folks, but don't worry, there's relief on the horizon!" The reporter would speak clearly and enunciate every syllable of every word. They would animate their voice to engage the audience and may even draw out certain key phrases like "but don't worry" to provide added reassurance and generate positive responses to their forecast. The weather reporter certainly would not speak the same way in more casual settings, like while having conversations at home.

To alter speech production in this manner involves manipulations at the suprasegmental level with changes in duration, intensity, and pitch, as described in Chapter 2. These alterations are based on the particular style of speech at hand, objectives of the interaction, and social dynamic between the interlocutors, among other factors. The academic and social space of the L2 classroom provides a unique speech scenario in which many variables affect the realization of prosody. This chapter outlines the main prosodic differences between formal and more casual speech styles, describes what we know about teacher talk in L2 classrooms and variation across teachers, and discusses relevant evidence from previous studies on similar speech styles.

Formal and informal speech

According to Labov (1972), informal speech contexts occur naturally and involve "casual" speech which is unmonitored and vernacular (p. 86). On the other hand, formal speech contexts are those in which speakers are being observed. When speakers are consciously aware that they are being observed, they use "careful" speech with more precise articulation and clearer enunciation. According to Labov, the paradox of sociolinguistic observation is that the informant's behavior is influenced by the presence of the observer; so, spontaneous speech occurs during formal speech only "when the constraints of formal speech are overridden" (p. 86), such as when the speaker is distracted by their emotions or other situational stimuli. Barry and Andreeva (2001) refine Labov's definition of spontaneous speech as that which is "unscripted, unprepared in terms of the number, organisation and expression of the information points it communicates" (p. 55).

For the analyses presented in this book, the participants were aware that they were being observed during the elicitation of speech data, so both conversational speech and SDS data represent formal speech. The speech elicited in both styles was unscripted, but both were in some ways planned, as the conversational speech was elicited using prompt questions and the teachers had planned their lessons ahead of time. Nevertheless, the discourse in both speech styles was largely spontaneous in terms of Barry and Andreeva's (2001) definition. The progression of the discourse and interactional exchanges such as talk turns were completely unprompted. That being said, due to the differences in speech context, it is expected that conversational speech will involve more casual, natural speech resembling the speakers' vernacular when compared to SDS, which will involve more careful speech given the proficiency differential between the speakers and listeners in addition to the various objectives of the FL classroom. Details about the speech environment in L2 classrooms is discussed later in this chapter.

Phonetic reduction

Phonetic weakening is common in informal speech and formal, spontaneous speech styles in all human languages, contrasting with the features of more careful speech styles where reduction is less frequent (Barry & Andreeva, 2001; Hualde, 2005). The acoustic phenomenon of reduction is realized in a variety of ways at both the segmental and suprasegmental levels, for example, the devoicing of voiced obstruents, the deletion of intervocalic approximants, and deaccenting of intonational contours (Aguilar, Blecua, Machuca, & Marín, 1993; Barry & Andreeva, 2001; Piñeros, 2002; Rao, 2009). This weakening is attributed mostly to time and ease of articulation and typically occurs in non-prominent positions. It is so pervasive in casual, connected speech among all speakers that it is often viewed as the "normal way to communicate" as opposed to a "sloppy" deviation from the norm (Warner & Tucker, 2011, p. 1615). However, in the L2 classroom, strengthening consonants can aid in word comprehension, phoneme to grapheme mapping, and sound discrimination, similar to the way adults speak to infants making sense of new auditory stimuli. While segmental strengthening in SDS is pertinent, the present investigation is concerned only with suprasegmental features of the speech style.

Declarative intonational contour patterns discussed previously are rather systematically observed in laboratory research; however, researchers have reported divergence from patterns in spontaneous speech where suprasegmental features are susceptible to reduction and strengthening phenomena (Face, 2003). An example of reduction in spontaneous speech is the suppression of F0 movement. Face (2003) compared declarative intonation in laboratory speech and spontaneous speech and found notable differences. F0 peak suppression was more common in spontaneous speech, suggesting that data elicitation methodology influences intonation. For example, Figure 3.1 displays an utterance, "*empecé a buscar otros canales que son como vlog*" 'I started to look for other channels that are like video blogs,' produced during Tammy's conversational speech data presented in this book. In this phrase, many of the words that are lexically specified to carry stress are deemphasized, and thus, are not accompanied by F0 peaks. According to Quilis' (1981) stressed word list, we would expect F0 movement in the word "*empecé*" 'I started,' but this is not the case.

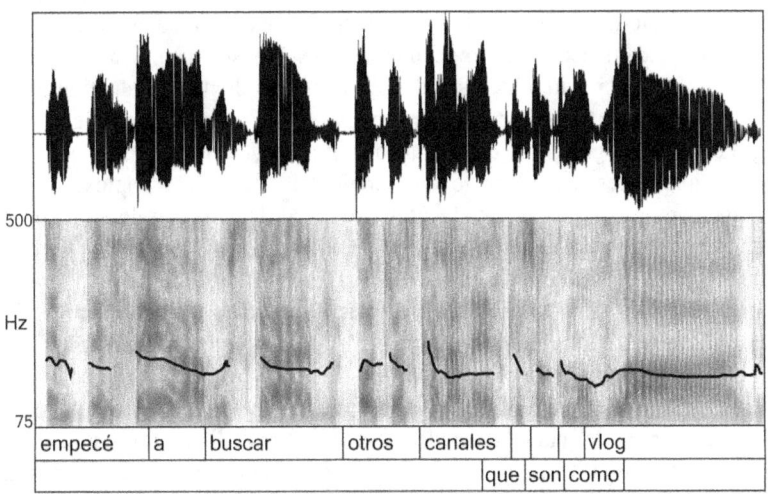

Figure 3.1 F0 suppression in conversation.

Face (2003) attributes F0 suppression to reduction processes at play during rapid articulation common to unmonitored, spontaneous speech. He explains that laboratory speech is elicited in a controlled setting, is often scripted, and is collected for the purpose of linguistic analysis, thus yielding speech that is more monitored by the speaker and less reduced. Given the presence of F0 suppression in spontaneous speech and not in laboratory speech in his study, Face maintains that laboratory speech is not a faithful representation of spontaneous speech. However, F0 suppression could also be a strategy used by the speaker to increase the salience of segments carrying special emphasis or narrow focus by suppressing non-focal accents, particularly post-focal accents (Beckman, Díaz-Campos, McGory, & Morgan, 2002; Face, 2003; Hualde, 2002; O'Rourke, 2012; Rao, 2009).

Data elicitation methodologies utilized in the present investigation yield speech that is as representative as possible of the speech produced in natural speech environments. Because reduction and strengthening phenomena differentiate conversational speech from SDS, and due to the special emphasis and narrow focus contexts pervasive in L2 classroom discourse, it is valuable to explore F0 suppression (or lack thereof) by teachers in the two speech contexts.

Extralinguistic factors involved in reduction

The use of reduction and strengthening varies among speakers according to speech style, objective of the speech act, and focus (Faraco, Kida, Barbier, & Piolat, 2002; Gerard & Dahan, 1995; Rao, 2011; Schilling, 2013). Sociolinguistic studies on reduction have pointed to differences among speakers according to gender and age. Ernestus and Warner (2011) found that men and older speakers use more phonetic reduction than women and younger speakers, respectively. Research examining social groups and geographical regions also found that the type and quantity of reduction varies according to environmental setting, the context of the speech act, the different interlocutors involved, and speech domains (oral or written) that are activated during an interaction (Ernestus & Warner, 2011; Hualde, 2005; Warner & Tucker, 2011). Additionally, phonetic strengthening occurs when there are environmental obstacles such as background noise, comprehension or interpretation of speech is inhibited, or the listener requires (or is perceived to require) special accommodations. Finally, speakers manipulate the relative prosodic strength of constituents to give perceptual cues to the listeners, such as to listen for a particular word or to pay attention for important information (Rao, 2006; Schilling, 2013). Rao (2006) identified emotional load as having the greatest impact, and that the speaker's attitude, the relevance of the information, and the

Didactic speech 33

communicative importance of the utterance also cause variation in reduction and strengthening.

Cruttenden (2007) described the oral speech of an English-speaking female in Glasgow and observed different intonational patterns according to speech style: falling intonation in conversational speech and rising intonation during read speech. He considered this finding to be justification for his case for "intonational diglossia," or the existence of "two distinct intonation systems" according to speech context (p. 257). However, speaking condition is not dichotomous. Warner and Tucker (2011) describe that "the effect of speech style is gradient, with conversational speech the most reduced, connected read speech the next most reduced, and words read in isolation least reduced" (p. 1615). In a formal setting, these different speech styles can be elicited using corresponding speech tasks, as seen in Figure 3.2,[1] that range on a continuum from less to more representative of spontaneous speech.

The present investigation was designed to minimize the effects of confounding extralinguistic variables on speech prosody, specifically regarding gender, age, emotion, attitude, and communicative importance. Quantitative and qualitative data are analyzed recursively in order to accomplish this goal.

Second language classroom discourse

In order to fully understand the inner workings of prosody during SDS as it occurs in L2 classrooms, it is crucial to first acknowledge the role of the teacher, review previous research on prosody in the didactic speech style, and discuss differences between individual teachers. For only a couple of hours a week, L2 students at the collegiate level are exposed to the target culture and language presented to them by means of their textbook, media supplements used in class or assigned for homework, and their teacher. Because their experiences with the TL are often confined to the classroom, the input to which students are exposed is mostly that of the teacher. So, if students build their language upon what they are exposed to during class,

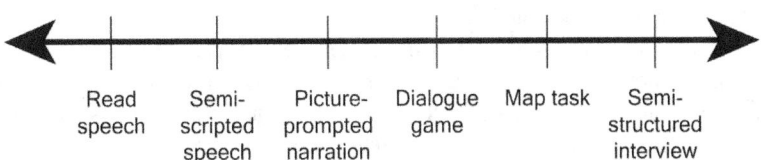

Figure 3.2 Speech elicitation tasks.

it is imperative to study oral speech behaviors of teachers in order to understand their effect on students.

Interactional discourse in the L2 classroom

Despite the importance of input for language development, very little attention has been paid to the unique variety of Spanish used by instructors in the language classroom. Eriks-Brophy and Crago (2003) cite several research studies that estimate that "teacher talk comprises two thirds of the total talk that occurs in classrooms" (p. 398), a total that warrants inquiry into the variety of language used by these speakers. However, speech acts cannot be examined without considering the wider social context in which the interaction is taking place. Discourse in the classroom is governed by the unique nature of this type of bilingual community and the hierarchical relationship between the teacher and students (McNeill, 2005).

The roles of teacher talk

Interactions in the L2 Spanish classroom often involve a steep differential in language proficiency and experience between the instructor and the students, and the discourse in this context commonly has an explicit didactic objective. Simultaneously acting as both class administrator and model of the TL, L2 teachers control the flow and interactions in the classroom, and students are at the mercy of their teachers' linguistic background and knowledge base (Cook, 1999; Walsh, 2013; Willis, 1992). The dual purpose of SDS was originally presented in Sinclair and Brazil's (1982) analysis of classroom discourse that categorizes segments of teacher talk as fulfilling either *inner* or *outer* purposes. Willis (1992) explains that inner refers to utterances that contain target forms, linguistic modeling of TL usage, or any language practice controlled by the teacher, and outer refers to utterances used for a pedagogic or administrative purpose, such as explaining an assignment, checking for comprehension, or organizing the class. Christie (2002) redefined these purposes as two types of registers: *instructional* is used to deliver a lesson's content and *regulative* is used for administrative purposes. Both Willis (1992) and Christie (2002) describe linguistic and paralinguistic cues associated with the inner, i.e., instructional, and outer, i.e., regulatory, registers. Willis explains that teachers provide students with cues through intonation, gestures, and other paralinguistic means to aid them in figuring out what they need to do to fulfill their duties in the class, and that these cues differ according to the speech function.

Additionally, SDS involves linguistic reduction processes referred to by some scholars as *language grading* (Thornbury & Watkins, 2007, p. 207) that are thought to have beneficial pedagogical effects on learners (Stanley & Stevenson, 2017; Thornbury & Watkins, 2007; Walsh, 2013). Stanley and Stevenson (2017) describe language grading in the classroom in terms of simplification of forms similar to the modified speech of caretakers and speech directed to foreigners. Walsh (2013) makes a similar comparison explaining that teachers use more of a "restricted code ... similar to the spoken language of parents talking to young children: it is typically slower, louder, more deliberate, and makes greater use of pausing and emphasis" (p. 31). According to Walsh, teachers use reduced vocabulary, fewer idiomatic expressions, simpler grammar, shorter utterances, more limited verbal inflections, clearer speech, and a slower articulation rate (p. 32).

Walsh (2013) holds that the vocal adjustments that occur during SDS are "conscious and deliberate" (p. 31) to facilitate comprehension and learning; however, there may also be subconscious physiological factors influencing teacher talk (Tobin, King, Henderson, Bellocchi, & Ritchie, 2016). In a unique investigation, Tobin et al. (2016) used mixed measures to learn about the expression of emotions while teaching and found that the participant in their study experienced a high heart rate and low blood oxygenation before and while teaching due to stress, which was associated with "confusing patterns in prosody, including intonation, pace of speaking, and pausing" (p. 669). Prosody was perceived as engaging when blood oxygenation was higher, which occurred while the participant was teaching. Identifying the physiological effects of teaching helps inform the interpretation of prosodic phenomena occurring during SDS. Additionally, education and training may be associated with the teachers' calmness and anxiety, which would have the physiological effects mentioned by Tobin et al.

The phrases extracted from the SDS analyzed in this book were coded by purpose according to Willis's (1992) and Christie's (2002) classifications of speech functions. SDS is likely to have the strengthening features that are characteristic of language grading (Stanley & Stevenson, 2017; Thornbury & Watkins, 2007; Walsh, 2013), and is likely to involve physiological reactions that affect speech at the prosodic level (Tobin et al., 2016). These observations are used to guide the interpretation of findings in the current investigation.

Prosody and intonation during student-directed speech

The role of prosody has been shown to be communicatively important in numerous experimental studies on SDS. In his study of classroom discourse analysis (DA), Hewings (1992) showed that teachers are able to express approval or disapproval, direct students' attention to an important target structure, and manage discourse of the classroom through pitch manipulations. Teachers in his study indicated the end of a statement with a L tone to signal that they were satisfied with a response or finished with an interaction. Similarly, through their analysis using conversation analysis (CA) of student-teacher interactions during an open-ended classroom discussion activity, Skidmore and Murakami (2012) found that teachers used emphatic speech to stress certain words and a slow pace of speech to mark the end of a substantive point.

In their exploration of emphatic accent during a classroom-based reading task, Gerard and Dahan (1995) found that speakers used slower speech immediately preceding a particularly relevant target-word. This finding corroborates segment lengthening as a feature of SDS and warrants a deeper look into the effect of context on duration. In another study on the use of prosody in SDS, Faraco et al. (2002) compared notetaking in learners' first language (L1) and L2. The participants heard a lecture that exhibited features of the "didactic accent" in French, which the authors defined as a slower pace, long silent initial and final pauses, voice projection (i.e., an increase in intensity), and the absence of hesitations (p. 1). The results of their study revealed that L2 learners took better notes when the teacher utilized auditory cues such as more pauses, higher intensity, and a slower speed of speech. They also found that advanced L2 students are more sensitive to prosodic cues than L1 students and are thus more capable of discerning relevant information than lower level L2 learners thanks to prosodic cues.

Rao (2011) elicited oral speech samples from NSs of Spanish in a laboratory setting and found that the speakers tended to use many of the features of formal or emphatic speech in the didactic style including an increased overall pitch range, early F0 peak alignment, boundary tones associated with communicatively important items, less F0 suppression, clear and gradual downstepping of less important phrases, higher intensity, and longer duration. Rao concluded that many of the acoustic correlates of didactic speech are consistent with reported phenomena used during teacher talk, most likely to facilitate L2 comprehension. For instance, teachers may use an increased F0 range for words or phrases that are particularly crucial to the students' understanding of a passage or to their ability to answer comprehension questions. However, it is possible that Rao's findings could be explained by the speech elicitation methodology used in his study. Face (2003) and O'Rourke (2012) caution that phenomena such as downstepping could be more pervasive in laboratory speech than natural speech. This observation merits careful investigation of these phenomena to gauge their prominence in naturally-occurring speech in L2 classrooms.

Due to the multitude of studies that point to the presence and importance of prosodic modifications made by L2 teachers to accommodate to their students and facilitate comprehension, it is important to perform quantitative studies that provide acoustic evidence of these phenomena. Furthermore, because of the evidence that prosodic adaptations are conscious, it may be possible to teach these skills with the end goal of improving teacher preparedness in terms of prosodic behavior (Tobin et al., 2016; Walsh, 2013). This pedagogical implication provides further justification for the explorations presented in this book.

Second language teacher variation

In our increasingly globalized world, more than half of the population is bilingual or multilingual, and this is the case as well with L2 teachers in the US. As with any group of human beings, the population of L2 teachers is heterogeneous, and the ways in which individuals vary are innumerable. Given the goals of this volume, the following sections focus mainly on how L2 teachers' identity as a bilingual language user influences the classroom dynamic. More specifically, because of the ongoing debate in the field of ISLA as to the relative efficacy of NS teachers versus NNS teachers, the variable of nativeness is of particular interest in this book and is discussed in this section. The perspectives of both teachers and students are considered.

Native and near-native speaker teachers

It is a common myth that NSs are better teachers than NNSs of a TL simply due to their NS status (Phillipson, 1992). In fact, many people assume that any NS of a language is automatically capable of teaching that language. This myth has been debunked over the years with research pointing out the virtues and shortcomings of teachers from different linguistic backgrounds (Árva & Medgyes, 2000; Beaudrie, 2009; Callahan, 2006; Canagarajah, 1999; Cook, 1999, 2016; Hertel & Sunderman, 2009; Medgyes, 1994; Samimy & Brutt-Griffler, 1999). Indeed, language use is not the same thing as language learning or language teaching (Widdowson, 1994). Canagarajah (1999) argues that not all people make effective teachers of their L1, but that competence in more than one language may be the key to success in language teaching, claiming that "proficiency in more than one language system develops a deep metalinguistic knowledge and complex language awareness" (p. 80). In observational investigations into nativeness of ESL teachers, Medgyes (1994) listed the following advantages of being a near-native speaker teacher (NNST) according to teachers' self-reports elicited through questionnaires.

38 *Didactic speech*

1   They are models of successful learners.
2   They are able to teach learning strategies based on their own learning experiences.
3   They have more keen metalinguistic awareness.
4   They have empathy for the L2 learning process.
5   They can predict where L2 learners will have difficulties.
6   They can use their L1 for teaching purposes.

Árva and Medgyes (2000) replicated these findings through their study analyzing ESL teachers in Budapest, Hungary. The authors enumerated both non-linguistic and linguistic differences between native speaker teachers (NSTs) and NNSTs according to data from questionnaires administered to teachers. The participants reported that NSTs had an advantage over NNSTs in terms of competency in the TL, but that NSTs were lacking with respect to meta-cognitive knowledge of grammar, competency in the societal majority language (Hungarian), and empathy for learning the TL. Empathy between NNSTs and their students was also demonstrated in Cots and Díaz's (2005) study showing that solidarity was expressed through the use of the pronoun *we*. McNeill (2005) compared NSTs and NNSTs of English in Hong Kong and found that the NNSTs were generally more successful in predicting students' lexical problems, showing that teachers who share an L1 with the students have an advantage in this area.

Because of the implication that nativeness affects numerous facets of L2 teaching, NS or NNS status is included as an independent variable in the present investigation.

Student perspectives

Relationships between teachers and students are also explored in studies on student perceptions of NSTs and NNSTs. In Samimy and Brutt-Griffler's study (1999), non-native English speaking graduate students working towards degrees in TESOL reported NSTs as being "informal, flexible, self-confident, fluent, and accurate users of English," and NNSTs as being "more sensitive to the students' needs, efficient, aware of negative transfer in learners' interlanguage, able to use learners' L2 as a medium, and tending to rely on textbooks" (p. 135). Other studies analyzing anecdotal evidence in the L2 Spanish setting show similar reports of student perceptions of teachers. The students in Callahan's (2006) study reported that they were able to identify better with NNSTs but were more comfortable speaking with NSTs. It is also a common perception that NNSTs are better at understanding learner challenges and teaching grammar and vocabulary while NSTs are better teachers of pronunciation and culture

(Callahan, 2006; Hertel & Sunderman, 2009). However, nativeness is not the only factor contributing to how students perceive teaching quality. The goals of the academic program, the students' age and proficiency levels, and the teacher's personality, qualifications, and teaching abilities also play important roles in students' evaluation of teaching effectiveness (Callahan, 2006; Cots & Díaz, 2005; Samimy & Brutt-Griffler, 1999).

In addition to considering the variable of TL nativeness, the present investigation takes into account the individual characteristics of the teaching assistants (TAs) and their descriptions of the classes they were teaching at the time of data collection in order to elucidate explanations for prosodic trends discovered in the data.

Accommodative speech styles and contexts

During SDS, teachers often use careful articulation and prosodic cues that engage listeners and direct their attention to important target features (Ernestus & Warner, 2011; Faraco et al., 2002; Gerard & Dahan, 1995; Hualde, 2007). We have evidence of this through impressionistic accounts and laboratory-based experimental data, but more empirical studies are needed to describe the actual prosodic realizations of SDS in language classrooms. From the knowledge we have, many scholars have compared the didactic speech type to other formal, accommodative speech types, most notably foreigner-directed speech (FDS), i.e., the speech directed to perceived foreigners, and infant-directed speech (IDS), i.e., the speech directed to young children. Findings from research into these speech types have implications that guide the study of SDS.

Speech accommodation

In any interactional environment, speakers will accommodate to the speech of their interlocutors (Gallois, Ogay, & Giles, 2005; Giles, 1973; Giles & Coupland, 1991). Giles's (1973) Speech Accommodation Theory (SAT) posited that speakers either converge to the "accent" (i.e., dialect or a particular pronunciation style) of their listeners or diverge from it based on underlying social or cognitive processes (p. 88). Giles and Coupland (1991) expanded upon this theory in their Communication Accommodation Theory (CAT) by incorporating the dimensions of non-verbal communication and interactional discourse, suggesting that interlocutors modify their speech, vocal patterns, and gestures to accommodate to one another. Another model that prioritizes the influence of social environment on speech production and discourse is Bell's (1984) Audience Design model. This model proposes that speech is shaped by its audience and that speakers adjust their speech to their listeners in order to gain acceptance and approval; however, it is important to note that these adjustments match the expected speech patterns of addressees and do not necessarily align with the addressees' actual speech patterns (Schilling, 2013).

The observations documented in these theories suggest that accommodations may be prevalent in the interactional L2 classroom, especially due to the hierarchal structure of the teacher-student dynamic in terms of language proficiency, knowledge, and authority. Given the importance of input in the L2 classroom, it is particularly valuable to inquire about the type and degree of linguistic accommodations in SDS, as well as how strategies are employed by different L2 teachers within the unique social spaces of their classrooms.

Foreigner-directed speech and infant-directed speech

Generally speaking, FDS and IDS both involve slow, clear articulation where speakers exaggerate the duration, intensity, pitch, and stress patterns of their speech, use a wider vowel space, and produce consonants more carefully and with less phonological reduction (Bergeson, Miller, & McCune, 2006; Kuhl et al., 1997; Scarborough, Brenier, Zhao, Hall-Lew, & Dmitrieva, 2007). Ferguson (1975) performed a corpus study with the end goal of developing a catalog of the linguistic features of FDS. The modifications he determined as qualities of FDS included grammatical omissions, expansions, rearrangements, and lexical substitutions. There is a bulk of research outlining the morphosyntactic and lexical properties of FDS similar to Ferguson's study, but a great deal of information about the linguistic qualities of careful, formal speech types has been revealed through studies on IDS. Kuhl et al. (1997) found that speakers produced more acoustically extreme vowels when speaking with infants in comparison to adults. There are also reports of hyperarticulation of consonants during IDS, where researchers have discovered more clearly articulated consonantal variants when compared to adult-directed speech (ADS).

Moving beyond the segmental level, Bergeson et al. (2006) compared prosodic characteristics of mothers addressing children who were either normal-hearing (NH) or hearing-impaired and had used a cochlear implant (CI) for three to 18 months. The researchers found that when addressing both NH and CI infants, mothers spoke with higher pitch, increased pitch range, shorter utterances with longer duration of individual words, and longer interutterance pauses. These correlates of IDS are consistent with findings from the majority of studies on the topic; however, other researchers have included higher amplitude (i.e., the distance between the maximum and minimum points of a waveform and its equilibrium, proportional to intensity and also perceived as loudness) and slower overall speech rate as characteristics of the speech type as well (Burnham, Gamache, Bergeson, & Dilley, 2013; Payne, Post, Astruc, Prieto, & Vanrell, 2009; Scarborough et al., 2007; Uther, Knoll, & Burnham, 2007; Warner & Tucker, 2011).

Prosodic modifications during IDS and FDS are believed to serve different functions, including to attract attention to language, highlight linguistic structures, aid in word identification, and emphasize phonological distinctions (Golinkoff, Can, Soderstrom, & Hirsh-Pasek, 2015; Kuhl et al., 1997; Payne et al., 2009). Kuhl et al. (1997) maintain that the exaggerated forms delivered to infants provide them with information about the sound system of the TL, more specifically, how to parse sounds into phonemically contrasting categories. These modified forms have the implicit objective of promoting language acquisition. Fernald (2000) explains that adults use IDS to highlight the aspects of speech that are important for learning syntactic structures.

Because SDS in L2 classrooms shares many of the same goals as FDS and IDS, the same prosodic correlates are likely responsible for prosodic adaptations in the different speech styles. Therefore, studies on FDS and IDS inform the design of the present investigation in several ways that are outlined in the rest of this section.

Methodological implications

Studies on FDS and IDS have revealed that the interactional context of a speech act has an effect on the outcome of data (Uther et al., 2007). In their study on accommodation strategies used during FDS, Scarborough et al. (2007) found differences when speakers were addressing real interlocutors compared to imaginary interlocutors. Speakers addressing imagined listeners produced slower speech with longer vowel sounds compared to speakers addressing real listeners. The researchers concluded that speech produced with imagined listeners is not representative of genuine FDS and is, therefore, not a valid data elicitation tool. They predicted that pitch mean and range are also skewed by elicitation tasks involving imagined interlocutors and urged future researchers to employ communicatively authentic tasks to measure real-world phenomena.[2]

Recent research has also pointed out differences between IDS and FDS that are relevant in order to accurately understand SDS. Biersack, Kempe, and Knapton (2005) compared CDS and FDS using ADS as a baseline. They found that while all speakers decreased their speech rate, they did so differently depending on their interlocutors. Participants increased the length of word segments when addressing an imaginary child but increased the length of pauses when addressing an imaginary foreigner. Participants also increased their pitch range and maximum pitch when addressing an imaginary child, but not when addressing an imaginary foreigner. These observed acoustic differences between CDS and FDS warrant further study on the acoustic correlates of SDS that may distinguish it from other listener-directed, formal speech types. For instance, Biersack et al. (2005) explained that pitch manipulation is an attention-eliciting strategy and is, therefore, detectable in CDS, but not necessarily detectable in FDS.

The implication that context affects speech prosody warrants future research that utilizes naturalistic data elicitation methodologies such as that presented in this book. Furthermore, the reported differences between CDS and FDS are particularly relevant to the present exploration because attention-elicitation (manifested as pitch manipulation) could be a component of classroom-based SDS depending on the learning context and interpersonal dynamic of the classroom.

Applied implications

The acoustic differences between CDS and FDS discovered in Biersack et al.'s (2005) study reveal that speakers are able to make prosodic modifications to accommodate to their listeners even when their listeners are imagined, thus suggesting that prosodic adaptations are learned and not merely inspired by listener feedback. This finding has implications with regard to L2 teacher education and training. If we are able to isolate the particular classroom speech modifications that are beneficial to learning, either by aiding in comprehension, increasing saliency, engaging learners, or in another way, we can teach future teachers to utilize these tools in their classrooms.

Finally, there is compelling research that ties clear speech input to improved speech development for infants, though the influence of didactic speech on L2 language acquisition needs more thorough examination (Burnham et al., 2013; Ernestus & Warner, 2011). There is strong evidence supporting the linguistic effects of IDS on the discrimination of sounds at an early age, and many researchers have positively correlated early language discrimination with enhanced language abilities later in life (Kuhl, Conboy, Padden, Nelson, & Pruitt, 2005). The outcome of clear speech input can also be seen through the potentially adverse effects of speech reduction. Ernestus and Warner (2011) assert that "reduced pronunciation variants have far reaching consequences for psycholinguistic models of speech production and comprehension, for language acquisition, and for speech technology" (p. 253).

The implication that prosodic adaptations are learned suggests that L2 teachers can improve their use of prosody to facilitate learning. Similarly, if clear speech and a decrease in reduction phenomena positively influence

Didactic speech 43

language acquisition during IDS, it is logical to assume that the same would occur in L2 contexts. These observations point to potential pedagogical benefits of research on SDS prosody.

Notes

1 The graphic in Figure 3.2 is based on data elicitation methodologies discussed in Face (2003) and Rao (2009).
2 This viewpoint supports the perspectives of Face (2003) but goes against those of Hualde (2002) with regard to the influence of the data elicitation environment on the type of speech elicited.

References

Aguilar, L., Blecua, B., Machuca, M., & Marín, R. (1993). Phonetic reduction processes in spontaneous speech. *Eurospeech*, 433–436. Retrieved from www.isca-speech.org/archive

Árva, V., & Medgyes, P. (2000). Native and non-native teachers in the classroom. *ScienceDirect*, *28*(3), 355–372. doi: 10.1016/S0346-251X(00)00017-8

Barry, W., & Andreeva, B. (2001). Cross-language similarities and differences in spontaneous speech patterns. *Journal of the International Phonetic Association*, 51–66. doi: 10.1017/S0025100301001050

Beaudrie, S. M. (2009). Teaching Spanish heritage learners and the nativeness issue. *ADFl Bulletin*, *4*(1), 94–112. doi: 10.1632/adfl.41.1.94

Beckman, M. E., Díaz-Campos, M., McGory, J. T., & Morgan, T. A. (2002). Intonation across Spanish, in the Tones and Break Indices framework. *Probus*, *14*(1), 9–36. doi: 10.1515/prbs.2002.008

Bell, A. (1984). Language style as audience design. *Language in Society*, *13*, 145–204. doi: 10.1017/S004740450001037X

Bergeson, T. R., Miller, R. J., & McCune, K. (2006). Mothers' speech to hearing-impaired infants and children with cochlear implants. *Infancy*, *10*(3), 221–240. doi: 10.1207/s15327078in1003_2

Biersack, S., Kempe, V., & Knapton, L. (2005). Fine-tuning speech registers: A comparison of the prosodic features of child-directed and foreigner-directed speech. *Interspeech*, 2401–2404. doi: 10.13140/2.1.2133.5049

Burnham, E., Gamache, J. L., Bergeson, T., & Dilley, L. (2013). Voice-onset time in infant-directed speech over the first year and a half. *Proceedings of Meetings on Acoustics ICA2013, Montreal*, *19*, 060094. doi: 10.1121/1.4800072

Callahan, L. (2006). Student perceptions of native and non-native speaker language instructors: A comparison of ESL and Spanish. *Sintagma*, *18*, 19–49. Retrieved from www.sintagma.udl.cat/en/

Canagarajah, S. (1999). Interrogating the "native-speaker fallacy": Non-linguistic roots, non-pedagogical results. In G. Braine (Ed.), *Non-native educators in English language teaching* (pp. 77–92). Mahwah, NJ: Lawrence Erlbaum. doi: 10.4324/9781315045368

Christie, F. (2002). *Classroom discourse analysis: A functional perspective.* London: Bloomsbury Publishing. doi: 10.1590/S0102-44502006000100012
Cook, V. (1999). Going beyond the native speaker in language teaching. *TESOL Quarterly, 33*(2), 185–209. doi: 10.2307/3587717
Cook, V. (2016). Where is the native speaker now? *TESOL Quarterly, 50*(1). doi: 10.1002/tesq.286
Cots, J. M., & Díaz, J. P. (2005). Constructing social relationships and linguistic knowledge through non-native-speaking teacher talk. In E. Llurda (Ed.), *Non-native language teachers: Perceptions, challenges and contributions to the profession* (pp. 107–128). New York, NY: Springer.
Cruttenden, A. (2007). Intonational diglossia: A case study of Glasgow. *Journal of the International Phonetic Association, 37*(2), 257–274. doi: 10.1017/S0025100307002915
Eriks-Brophy, A., & Crago, M. (2003). Variation in instructional discourse features: Cultural or linguistic? Evidence from Inuit and non-Inuit teachers of Nunavik. *Anthropology and Education Quarterly, 34*(4), 396–419. doi: 10.1525/aeq.2003.34.4.396
Ernestus, M., & Warner, N. (2011). An introduction to reduced pronunciation variants. *Journal of Phonetics*, 253–260. doi: 10.1016/S0095-4470(11)00055-6
Face, T. L. (2003). Intonation in Spanish declaratives: Difference between lab speech and spontaneous speech. *Catalan Journal of Linguistics*, 115–131. Retreived from https://revistes.uab.cat/catJL
Faraco, M., Kida, T., Barbier, M. L., & Piolat, A. (2002). Didactic prosody and notetaking in L1 and L2. In *Speech Prosody 2002, International Conference.*
Ferguson, C. A. (1975). Toward a characterization of English foreigner talk. *Anthropological Linguistics, 1*(17), 1-14.
Fernald, A. (2000). Speech to infants as hyperspeech: Knowledge-driven processes in early word recognition. *Phonetica, 57*, 242–254. doi: 10.1159/000028477
Gallois, C., Ogay, T., & Giles, H. (2005). Communication accommodation theory: A look back and a look ahead. In W. Gudykunst (Ed.), *Theorizing about intercultural communication* (pp. 121–148). Thousand Oaks, CA: Sage.
Gerard, C., & Dahan, D. (1995). Durational variations in speech and didactic accent during reading. *Speech Communication, 16*(3), 293–311. doi: 10.1016/0167-6393(94)00060-N
Giles, H. (1973). Accent mobility: A model and some data. *Anthropological Linguistics, 15*(2), 87–105.
Giles, H., & Coupland, N. (1991). *Language: Contexts and consequences.* Milton Keynes: Open University Press.
Golinkoff, R. M., Can, D. D., Soderstrom, M., & Hirsh-Pasek, K. (2015). (Baby) talk to me: The social context of infant-directed speech and its effects on early language acquisition. *Association for Psychological Science, 24*(5), 339–344. doi: 10.1177/0963721415595345
Hertel, T., & Sunderman, G. (2009). Student attitudes toward native and non-native language instructors. *Foreign Language Annals, 42*, 468–482. doi: 10.1111/j.1944–9720.2009.01031.x

Hewings, M. (1992). Intonation and feedback in the EFL classroom. In M. Coulthard (Ed.), *Advances in spoken discourse analysis* (pp. 183–196). London: Routledge. doi: 10.1017/S0047404500017930

Hualde, J. I. (2002). Intonation in Spanish and the other Ibero-Romance languages: Overview and status quaestionis. In C. Wiltshire, & J. Camps (Eds.), *Romance philology and variation* (pp. 101–115). Philadelphia, PA: John Benjamins. doi: 10.1075/cilt.217.10hua

Hualde, J. I. (2005). *The sounds of Spanish.* Cambridge: Cambridge University Press. doi: 10.1017/CBO9780511719943

Hualde, J. I. (2007). Stress removal and stress addition in Spanish. *Journal of Portuguese Linguistics*, 59–89. doi: 10.5334/jpl.145

Kuhl, P. K., Conboy, B. T., Padden, D., Nelson, T., & Pruitt, J. (2005). Early speech perception and later language development: Implications for the "critical period". *Language Learning and Development, 1*(3-4), 237-264. doi: 10.1080/15475441.2005.9671948

Kuhl, P. K., Andruski, J. E., Chistovich, I. A., Chistovich, L. A., Kozhevnikova, E. V., Ryskina, V. L., Stolyarova, E. I., Sundberg, U., & Lacerda, F.(1997). Cross-language analysis of phonetic units in language addressed to infants. *Science, 277*(5326), 684–686. doi: 10.1126/science.277.5326.684

Labov, W. (1972). *Sociolinguistic patterns.* Philadelphia, PA: University of Pennsylvania Press.

McNeill, A. (2005). Non-native speaker teachers and awareness of lexical difficulty in pedagogical texts. In E. Llurda (Ed.), *Non-native language teachers: perceptions, challenges, and contributions to the profession* (pp. 107–128). doi: 10.1007/0-387-24565-0_7

Medgyes, P. (1994). *The non-native teacher.* London: Macmillan.

O'Rourke, E. (2012). The realization of contrastive focus in Peruvian Spanish intonation. *Lingua,* 494–510. doi: 10.1016/j.lingua.2011.10.002

Payne, E., Post, B., Astruc, L., Prieto, P., & Vanrell, M. (2009). Rhythmic modification in child directed speech. *Oxford University Working Papers in Linguistics, Philology & Phonetics,* 123–144. Retrieved from www.ling-phil.ox.ac.uk/files/uploads/OWP2009.pdf

Phillipson, R. (1992). *Linguistic imperialism.* Oxford: Oxford University Press. doi: 10.1002/9781405198431.wbeal0718.pub2

Piñeros, C. (2002). Markedness and laziness in Spanish obstruents. *Lingua,* 379–413. doi: 10.1016/S0024-3841(01)00048-1

Quilis, A. (1981). *Fonética acústica de la lengua española.* Madrid: Gredos.

Rao, R. (2006). On intonation's relationship with pragmatic meaning in Spanish. *Proceedings of the 8th Hipanic Linguistics Symposium* (pp. 103–115). Somerville, MA: Cascadilla Press.

Rao, R. (2009). Deaccenting in spontaneous speech in Barcelona Spanish. *Studies in Hispanic and Lusophone Linguistics, 2*(1), 31–75. doi: 10.1515/shll-2009-1035

Rao, R. (2011). Intonation in Spanish classroom-style didactic speech. *Journal of Teaching and Research, 3,* 31–75. doi: 10.4304/jltr.2.3.493-507

Samimy, R., & Brutt-Griffler, J. (1999). To be a native or non-native speaker: Perceptions of "nonnative" students in a graduate TESOL program. In G. Braine

(Ed.), *Nonnative educators in English language teaching* (pp. 127–144). Mahwah, NJ: Lawrence Erlbaum. doi: 10.4324/9781315045368

Scarborough, R., Brenier, J., Zhao, Y., Hall-Lew, L., & Dmitrieva, O. (2007). An acoustic study of real and imagined foreigner-directed speech. In J. Trouvain, & W. J. Barry (Eds.), *Proceedings of the 16th International Conference of the Phonetic Sciences* (pp. 2165–2168). Saarbruecken, Germany. doi: 10.1121/1.4781735

Schilling, N. (2013). Investigating stylistic variation. In J. K. Chambers, & N. Schilling (Eds.), *The handbook of language variation and change* (2nd ed., pp. 325–349). Hoboken, NJ: Wiley-Blackwell. doi: 10.1002/9781118335598.ch15

Sinclair, J. M., & Brazil, D. (1982). *Teacher talk*. London: Oxford University Press.

Skidmore, D., & Murakami, K. (2012). Claiming our own space: Polyphony in teacher-student dialogue. *Linguistics and Education, 23*, 200–210. doi: 10.1016/j.linged.2012.02.003

Stanley, P., & Stevenson, M. (2017). Making sense of not making sense: Novice English language teacher talk. *Linguistics and Education*, 1–10. doi: 10.1016/j.linged.2017.01.001

Thornbury, S., & Watkins, P. (2007). *The CELTA course: Trainee book*. Cambridge: Cambridge University Press. doi: 10.1093/elt/ccn031

Tobin, K., King, D., Henderson, S., Bellocchi, A., & Ritchie, S. M. (2016). Expression of emotions and physiological change during teaching. *Cultural Studies of Science Education, 11*, 669–692. doi: 10.1007/s11422-016-9778-9

Uther, M., Knoll, M. A., & Burnham, D. (2007). Do you speak E-NG-L-I-SH? A comparison of foreigner- and infant- directed speech. *Speech Communication*, 2–7. doi: 10.1016/j.specom.2006.10.003

Walsh, S. (2013). *Classroom discourse and teacher development*. Edinburgh: Edinburgh University Press. doi: 10.3366/j.ctt1g0b484.6

Warner, N., & Tucker, B. V. (2011). Phonetic variability of stops and flaps in spontaneous and careful speech. *Acoustical Society of America*, 1606–1617. doi: 10.1121/1.3621306

Widdowson, H. (1994). The ownership of English. *TESOL Quarterly, 28*, 377–389. doi: 10.2307/3587438

Willis, J. (1992). Inner and outer: Spoken discourse in the language classroom. In M. Coulthard (Ed.), *Advances in spoken discourse analysis* (pp. 162–182). London: Routledge. doi: 10.4324/9780203200063

4 Participants and procedures

Introduction

Evidence suggests that speech accommodations are pervasive in the L2 classroom, likely due to the competing functions and objectives of teacher talk and the social implications of the teacher–student dynamic (Christie, 2002; Giles & Coupland, 1991; Hualde, 2007; Stanley & Stevenson, 2017; Walsh, 2013). A teacher's use of prosody is also influenced by their individual style as well as their linguistic background and professional preparation (Árva & Medgyes, 2000; Callahan, 2006; Medgyes, 1994; Schilling, 2013). However, our knowledge about L2 teachers is largely based on research involving non-empirical reflections, personal narratives, surveys, interviews, and classroom observations, and there is a need for studies employing experimental or quasi-experimental designs that involve more rigorous practices such as objective measurements of performance indicators in the classroom (Llurda, 2014; Moussu & Llurda, 2008). The present investigation fills this gap by employing a mixed-methods approach that combines qualitative data gathered through questionnaires, interviews, and retrospection with quantitative data collected through direct acoustic measurements and backed by statistical tests.

Additionally, research studies to date that involve acoustic analysis of didactic speech have utilized laboratory data where stimuli were acoustically manipulated to mimic real speech or where participants were asked to read passages or speak in different styles. Laboratory data is more logistically feasible and practical, but more importantly, it is a more controlled, formal environment for valid data collection (Face, 2003). Despite the benefits of laboratory data, speech elicited in this environment does not necessarily resemble spontaneous speech that occurs in naturalistic settings (Face, 2003; O'Rourke, 2012). For this reason, the SDS samples collected in the present investigation were elicited from within real language classrooms during regularly scheduled classes taught by the participants.[1]

The conversational speech samples were elicited through small group conversations without the presence of an observer or interviewer (other than microphones), and the participants spoke freely at their own will. The findings reveal prosodic features of SDS while also shedding light on the compatibility between laboratory and naturalistic classroom data.

It is also important to expand the sample population used in studies on SDS to include speakers with different types of linguistic experiences and professional training. Most studies have explored the linguistic phenomena used by speakers classified as NSs of the TL, but as we all know, L2 teachers come from a wide range of linguistic backgrounds, and many researchers have noted differences between the practices of NSTs and NNSTs, as well as the way different teachers are perceived by students (Árva & Medgyes, 2000; Callahan, 2006; Canagarajah, 1999; Cook, 1999, 2016; Hertel & Sunderman, 2009; Medgyes, 1994; Samimy & Brutt-Griffler, 1999). The reported linguistic differences between NSTs and NNSTs necessitate a closer look at prosodic behaviors in the classroom. The current investigation uses information about the participants' language background both as a dependent variable and descriptively when interpreting how they utilize prosody in the classroom. Additionally, to help explain variation, the TAs reported information about their training and professional experiences.

Furthermore, to date, studies on didactic speech styles have primarily used cross-sectional designs, where researchers sample from a population and collect data at one specific point in time. When considering the ever-changing L2 classroom dynamic, we must account for how phonetic modifications are used at different times in the academic semester. For instance, it is possible that prosodic adaptations change throughout the semester as the teacher becomes more familiar with the students (and vice versa) and as the students' comprehension abilities improve. A longitudinal framework allows researchers to observe if and how these changes occur. The present research utilized audio data from three different points in the semester to gauge its influence on prosody, and time in the semester is treated as an orthogonal variable in the data analysis, i.e., a variable that is independent from other variables.

In order to fulfill these objectives, the following research questions were addressed:

1 What are the prosodic features of SDS as it occurs in intermediate L2 Spanish classrooms in the university context?
2 How, if at all, do prosodic variations between TAs correspond with their identity as native or near-native speakers of the target language or their professional training and experience?

3   How, if at all, do TAs adapt their prosodic patterns over the course of an academic semester?

Description of participants

Four participants were selected from the pool of TAs teaching third semester Spanish at a large Midwestern research university.[2] The motivation for using third semester Spanish instructors stems from personal experience teaching beginner and intermediate courses at the university level. In first semester Spanish classes, students have little to no prior experience with the TL, and the classroom is often the students' sole exposure to the language. Due to beginner L2 students' limited comprehension and proficiency, it is understandable that instructors would rely on the use of emphatic language and exaggerated vocal gestures in order to make themselves comprehensible to the students. Indeed, these are the very features under examination here; however, at these very preliminary stages of L2 development, the features of SDS likely closely resemble those of FDS and may even be inextricable from them. Also, L2 instruction at beginner levels typically involves instances of code-switching to increase comprehensibility or signal pedagogical focus (Olson & Ortega-Llebaria, 2010; Üstünel & Seedhouse, 2005). Contrastingly, in intermediate-level courses, students arrive with prior exposure to the TL either through L2 courses or personal experience with the TL at home or in the community. Although comprehension and proficiency levels of students in intermediate L2 courses are largely heterogeneous, it is generally assumed that these students have at least preliminary levels of comprehension; therefore, it is expected that in intermediate courses, linguistic accommodations at the prosodic level are prevalent but not as pervasive as in beginner courses.

Recruitment of participants was limited to female TAs between the ages of 23 and 30 who had been assigned to teach third semester Spanish during the semester of the collection of in-class speech samples. Participants of similar gender and age were enlisted for the sake of logistical ease as well as to enable acoustic comparisons between participants. Due to the effects that biological factors have on F0 production, keeping gender and age as constant as possible facilitates the input and analysis of pitch (Chun, 2002; Gussenhoven, 2002; Ohala, 1984). Even though the average pitch range tends to be similar among female speakers, the natural pitch registers of the individuals contributing to this research varied, so small adjustments were made in the pitch settings in Praat between speakers in order to optimize visualization of the pitch contours and wave frequencies.[3] Also, because age influences vocal anatomy, the chosen speakers were of similar age. Controlling for these variables also facilitated the interpretation of inter-participant comparisons. Even though the quantitative component of this analysis mostly involves a within-subject design in which the same group of participants are the subjects of two separate experimental conditions, comparisons across participants are useful when exploring if and how the individuals' linguistic, educational, and professional backgrounds interplay with their prosodic behavior.

In addition to age and gender, the NS or NNS speaker status of the participants was controlled for throughout this investigation. L2 teachers form a heterogeneous population of individuals including monolinguals, bilinguals, and multilinguals, but despite this reality, previous studies looking at SDS have typically involved NS informants. Broadening the scope of participants to include Spanish L2 teachers with different linguistic experiences provides a more faithful demographic representation of the modern population. Additionally, there are plenty of noteworthy differences between NSTs and NNSTs regarding knowledge, use of the TL, teaching style, and classroom practices (Árva & Medgyes, 2000; Canagarajah, 1999; Cook, 1999, 2016; Medgyes, 1994). It is now vital to observe for prosodic differences between teachers according to their NS and NNS status. To accomplish this task, the speech of both NSTs and NNSTs was analyzed, and linguistic status was treated as an independent variable in the present investigation.

After identifying candidates that fit the course assignment, age, gender, and NS/NNS status requirements, the researcher sent individual recruitment emails describing the research and discussing how the individuals would be involved if they chose to participate. Communication with the prospective participants continued through email until confirming the participation of two NS and two NNS female TAs teaching intermediate Spanish. The participants completed informed consent paperwork and a background questionnaire about their linguistic upbringing and experience, language use at the time of the data collection, and educational and professional experience. The questionnaire elicited self-reports of the participants' experiences and skills, an elicitation methodology that is recommended in research involving bilingual language use (Torres Cacoullos & Travis, 2013). Biographical information based on responses to the background questionnaire is outlined in Table 4.1 and Table 4.2.[4]

Data collection procedures

Because of the implication that prosodic modifications are amplified or take on different characteristics altogether in real-world settings when compared to imaginary settings (Biersack, Kempe, & Knapton, 2005; Face, 2003; Scarborough, Brenier, Zhao, Hall-Lew, & Dmitrieva, 2007;

Table 4.1 Biographical data

TA	City or state and country of origin	Age at time of data collection	Age of first exposure to Spanish	Age of first exposure to English	Length of time living in US at time of data collection	Level and subfield of graduate study
Lola	Valladolid, Spain	24	0	7	5 months	MA, Spanish literature and linguistics
Alejandra	Canary Islands, Spain	29	0	8	5 months	MA, Spanish literature and linguistics
Kate	Arizona, US	30	8	0	N/A	PhD, Spanish literature
Tammy	Wisconsin, US	29	12	0	N/A	PhD, Spanish literature

Table 4.2 Experience and educational background

TA	Teacher certified?	General teaching experience or training prior to starting at host institution?	Experience teaching Spanish as an L2 prior to starting at host institution?	Amount of time teaching Spanish at host institution at time of data collection	Number of semesters teaching intermediate course at host institution at time of data collection
Lola	No	No	No	<1 year	1
Alejandra	No	Yes	Yes	<1 year	1
Kate	No	Yes	No	>5 years	8
Tammy	No	No	No	>5 years	5

Uther, Knoll, & Burnham, 2007), the current investigation is based on audio samples isolating the instructors' speech that were collected from within real Spanish L2 classrooms. In order to compare the individuals' prosodic behaviors during SDS with their natural, conversational speech behaviors, the participants engaged in recorded conversations with their colleagues during small focus group interviews. This data provided a baseline for each participant used to distinguish between their idiosyncratic prosodic behaviors and the effect of speech style on their use of prosody in the two speech contexts.

In-class data collection

In order to capture the TAs' natural prosodic behaviors as teachers, the researcher recorded three regularly scheduled 50-minute classes for each participant at three times throughout the 15-week semester: the first at week three, the second at week seven, and the third at week 10. The classes were recorded using Olympus digital audio recorders, and the instructors wore small, individual microphones on their clothes a fixed distance from their mouths. Participants wore the microphones rather than having them in a static location in the room because, according to acoustic studies, the placement of recording devices relative to the speaker can have dramatic effects on the measurement of intensity, one of the correlates under observation in the present investigation (Hirst, 2006). With a body microphone, the instructors were able to move around freely without compromising the validity of acoustic measurements.

The four research participants were teaching the same intermediate Spanish course and using the same textbook, *Exploraciones: Curso Intermedio*, published by Cengage (Blitt, Casas, & Copple, 2013). While they were following the same syllabus and course calendar, each TA had the autonomy to create their own daily instructional lesson plans and choose the activities they administered in class. Therefore, while the content covered in each instructors' classes was generally the same, the daily lesson plans varied regarding teaching methods, activities, and classroom discourse. The recordings generally occurred on the same calendar days, and to make sure that the recorded classes would involve ample amounts of teacher talk, the chosen days were scheduled to involve vocabulary or grammar instruction and practice as opposed to silent in-class writing, for example. A description of the coursework covered on recorded days is included in Table 4.3. Nevertheless, despite efforts to minimize any confounding variables potentially influencing the comparability of the SDS samples, each lesson was unique as variability is inevitable in naturally-occurring speech.

Table 4.3 Curricular information

Day	Week in semester (out of 16)	Textbook chapter	Topics covered during recorded lessons
1	3rd	2: *Costumbres, tradiciones y valores* ('Customs, Traditions, and Values')	Chapter vocabulary presentation and practice Discussions of celebrations and holidays in the Hispanic world Review of the preterit and imperfect tenses Formal and informal commands
2	7th	4: *Héroes y villanos* ('Heroes and Villains')	Chapter vocabulary presentation and practice Discussions of historical figures and events in the Hispanic world Present subjunctive and imperfect subjunctive modes
3	10th	5: *Sociedades en transición* ('Societies in Transition')	Discussions of culturally relevant topics such as the effect of modern advances in our society, immigration, and social justice Present perfect tenses in the subjunctive mode Use of the subjunctive mode in adverbial clauses Preparation for oral interviews

Participants and procedures 55

All participants reported using Spanish 75–100% of the time while teaching, and Spanish was indeed the majority language used during the recorded classes. English was used minimally by all four participants, but more so by Lola and Alejandra, the two NSs of Spanish. In their case, English was used most frequently either to gloss words, clarify a misunderstanding (usually associated with administrative functions or abstract concepts), or provide in-depth feedback. For instance, Alejandra clarified the rules of Bingo in Spain compared to the US and Lola gave students individualized feedback in English on the practice oral interview they performed for her.

Semi-structured focus group interviews

The participants engaged in 45-minute focus group interviews in order to elicit natural conversational speech which serves as a baseline of prosodic behavior for each individual. Focus group interviews are a recommended methodology for eliciting more spontaneous, vernacular speech when compared to one-on-one interviews (Harding, 2013; Schilling, 2013). They involve interactions between group members instead of between a respondent and an interviewer. Participants engaged in the focus groups in pairs; these were arranged by native speaker status in order to eliminate the potential that speakers would accommodate to the language of their interlocutors. Conveniently, the grouping was also advantageous to the experiment because the members of each pair were friends and colleagues who interacted regularly in both academic and social settings. Familiarity between the members of the focus groups increased the likelihood that they would feel comfortable and produce natural, spontaneous speech despite the presence of audio recording equipment (Labov, 1972). To spark conversation, the groups received a list of discussion questions ranging from mundane topics to more poignant and polemic topics. They could talk about television programs, the importance of family, the value of education, the legalization of marijuana, or the ethics of the death penalty, for example. Participants wore individual voice-recorders and were asked to engage in regular conversation about whichever topics interested them. A facilitator of comparable linguistic background also participated in the conversations and was instructed to keep the conversation flowing if necessary.

Follow-up one-on-one interviews

As a follow-up to the data collection, the researcher met with each participant individually approximately two years after the recording of the SDS and conversational speech samples.[5] In the follow-up interviews, a retroactive protocol analysis utilizing stimulated recall was administered in order to address the questions of TA awareness of linguistic modifications during didactic speech and intentions for utilizing them. The researcher replayed recorded segments from the TAs' SDS samples and asked broad, general questions to avoid leading the participants, such as the following: What are you doing in this recording that you wouldn't do if you were speaking to a friend? Would you speak this way in any other situations? When you are speaking to the students, what are your main objectives? What kind of dynamic do you try to create in the classroom? Questions of this nature allowed participants to form an unbiased observation and assessment of their own teaching.

The results of these short interviews provide further insight into the source of SDS prosody in the classroom. For instance, if teachers are using prosodic modifications intentionally with a specific purpose, they may be described as a teaching practice with a pedagogical goal and, therefore, would be candidates for inclusion in teacher training programs. On the other hand, if teachers are unaware of their phonetic modifications or have no particular intention for employing them, the modifications may be due to conscious or subconscious accommodation to the listeners, features of careful or public speech, or expressions of discourse information or pragmatic meaning (Christie, 2002; Ernestus & Warner, 2011; Faraco, Kida, Barbier, & Piolat, 2002; Gerard & Dahan, 1995; Hualde, 2007; Rao, 2006, 2011; Schilling, 2013; Tobin, King, Henderson, Bellocchi, & Ritchie, 2016; Walsh, 2013).

Data input, coding, and analysis

Praat acoustic analysis software (Boersma & Weenink, 2016) was used to explore and analyze the data. Because speech was unscripted and spontaneous, the process of extracting and coding tokens was emergent and often involved adding or merging factors, recoding entire factor groups, and adding variables as new factor groups. Because there was a singular rater involved in data processing, several measures were taken to ensure methodological consistency and minimize biases. A series of statistical tests using SAS Studio 3.6 software allowed for further exploration of the significance of trends in the data.

Extraction of SDS and conversational speech tokens

Speech was parsed into measurable phrasal units according to a series of criteria. The first 600 seconds of each recording were discarded in order to minimize any possible effects of "observer's paradox" (Labov, 1972). Only declarative phrases uttered in the target language were extracted for a total of 600 SDS phrasal tokens, 150 per teacher, and 400 phrasal tokens of conversational speech, 100 per participant. Phrases containing more than 50% English words were eliminated; however, a few instances of code-switching or reference to proper nouns in English were present in both speech styles for every speaker and did not preclude the phrase's inclusion in the data sample. Tags and perturbations such as ¿vale? 'ok?', ¿sí? 'yes?', eh 'um', or o sea 'like' were discarded from the data when they were in isolation or at the beginning or end of a phrase.

Phrasing is logistically challenging when working with spontaneous speech styles because phrase boundaries can be marked in several different ways in Spanish, such as through pre-boundary lengthening, falling or rising BPM, pitch reset, or pauses (Estebas Vilaplana & Prieto, 2008; Prieto, 2006). Traditional chunking methods such as using t-units, i.e., measuring phrases as the shortest grammatically allowable sentence (Gut, Trouvain, & Barry, 2007), and relying solely on pauses were impractical for the present analysis due to the inconsistency in phrase types and the high frequency of pauses and perturbations (Chun, 2002; Face, 2001). Therefore, a combination of strategies was utilized to systematically parse speech data into phrases and maximize comparability between data sets. The following list enumerates the criteria that were used in the phrasal segmentation method employed by the researcher.

1 A phrase could be as small as one word, but due to logistical constraints associated with acoustic visualization in Praat, phrases could not exceed 10 seconds in duration.
2 The three primary factors delineating a phrase were a pause greater than 350 ms,[6] a change in sentence type (declarative or interrogative) or interlocutor, and a phrase boundary cue. A phrase boundary cue was identified by pre-boundary lengthening or extreme F0 movement at the end of a phrase.
3 If a phrase was longer than 10 seconds and did not include any of the aforementioned criteria, the phrase was parsed into segments based on the presence of short pauses between words, embedded tags or perturbations, or syntactic boundary markers such as conjunctive adverbs or transitional phrases.

Coding of SDS and conversational speech tokens

Once each phrase was extracted, a series of measurements of different prosodic features were taken in order to address the research questions.

For each phrasal token in both speech styles, duration, mean intensity, F0 mean, F0 minimum, and F0 maximum were measured. Speech rate was determined by dividing the number of syllables in a phrase by the total duration of the phrase in seconds, and F0 range accounted for the difference between minimum and maximum F0 values. Other factor groups coded in the data included the frequency of F0 peaks, pre-nuclear F0 rise pattern, and BPM pattern.

To account for the frequency of F0 peaks in phrases, four factors were created: phrases containing no pitch movement,[7] phrases containing 1 to 3 peaks, phrases containing 3 to 6 peaks, and those containing more than 6 peaks. This method facilitated the coding of this factor group because due to the spontaneous speech style, it was difficult at times to count the exact number of peaks in a phrase without exhaustive scrutiny, and it was unnecessary to have a precise count for the purposes of this investigation in any case. However, to account for the varying length of phrases across the two speech styles, a new variable was created by dividing the number of F0 peaks in each phrase by its duration. In the categorization of pre-nuclear F0 rise patterns, six factors were coded: absence of a peak pattern (e.g., cases of F0 suppression), downstepped F0 peaks (typical of broad focus declaratives), rise pattern associated with special prominence (e.g., target vocabulary words or narrow focus), upstepped F0 peaks, erratic F0 peaks (i.e., irregular peaks of varying height with no observable pattern), and hyper regular F0 peaks (i.e., several peaks of uniform height).

Finally, BPM patterns coded in the data were as follows: the absence of BPM, falling BPM, rising BPM, and high-rising BPM. A rise of 40% or more of the F0 mean of the phrase was considered a high-rising BPM, while a rise of less than 40% was considered rising BPM regardless of the pitch register of the tonal onset (Inoue, 2006). Because it was discovered in early stages of the data analysis that the frequency of high-rising and falling boundary movement were of particular interest, a new dichotomous variable was created for each of the aforementioned factors in order to isolate the effect of speech style on BPM shape. For instance, to look at the high-rising BPM pattern, the researcher recoded the factor group to be dichotomous, with high-rising BPM in one group and all other BPM shapes (no BPM, falling, and rising) in the other. Figure 4.1 displays examples of BPM shapes, all produced by Alejandra during SDS on the second day of recording. The word "*suerte*" 'luck' is not accompanied by BPM, "*Cortés*" 'Cortés' is followed by falling BPM, "*esto*" 'this' was produced with rising BPM, and "*Gerónimo de Aguilar*" 'Gerónimo de Aguilar' shows high-rising BPM.

Additional information was recorded for the SDS samples in order to shed light on the prosodic features unique to the speech style. Because of the many communicative and pragmatic functions of SDS (Christie, 2002;

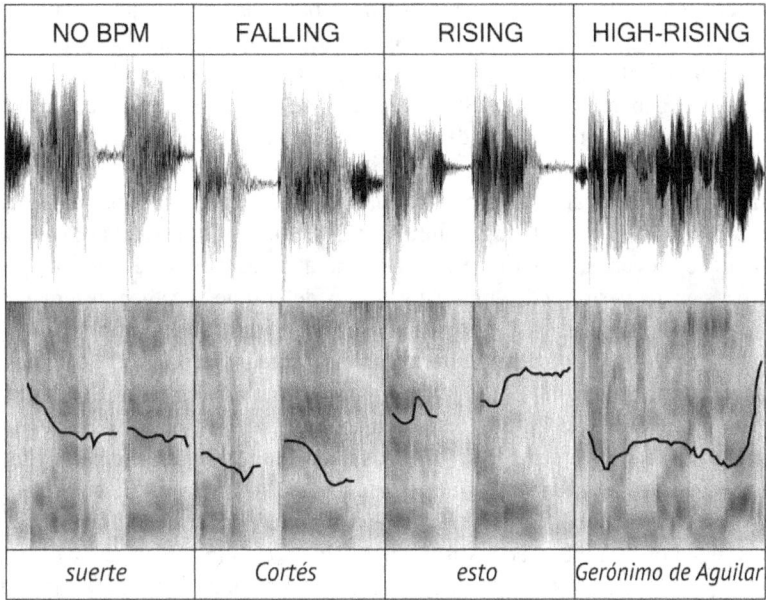

Figure 4.1 BPM shapes.

Willis, 1992), and due to the evidence that prosodic cues are involved in fulfilling such functions (Golinkoff, Can, Soderstrom, & Hirsh-Pasek, 2015; Payne, Post, Astruc, Prieto, & Vanrell, 2009; Kuhl et al., 1997), the phrases were coded for purpose including the following factors: neutral, read speech or activity prompt, modeled language or repetitions (including repetition of correct responses as well as response-seeking statements), repair or recast of student response, and instructions or administration (including discussion of content and grammar explanations). SDS tokens were also coded to denote whether or not they contained target words or phrases (i.e., a vocabulary word or phrase from the textbook chapter or grammatical form relevant to instruction). This information is used to determine the influence of communicatively important target words or phrases over the prosodic realizations used in the classroom.

Analysis of data

A within-subject design was employed to compare prosodic measurements across the two speech styles for each individual TA. According to

Charness, Gneezy, and Kuhn (2011), a within-subject design can minimize errors related to subject-level differences because each subject serves as their own baseline. For categorical variables (i.e., pre-nuclear F0 peak pattern, BPM, high-rising BPM, falling BPM), frequency distributions revealed general trends in SDS compared to conversational speech, and chi-square tests of independence were used to determine whether the differences according to speech style for each TA could be considered statistically significant. For continuous variables (i.e., articulation rate, intensity, F0 mean, F0 range, and F0 peak frequency), measures of central tendency revealed patterns in the data, and a series of independent sample t-tests were performed within-subjects to determine whether differences across the two speech styles could be attributed to chance alone.

Between-subject analyses were also performed on variables of interest according to the results of the within-subject analyses in order to identify significant prosodic differences across speech styles overall. A series of linear mixed effects models (LMEMs) accounted for fixed effects (i.e., speech style) and random effects (i.e., subject and time in the semester). Mixed effects models provide accurate estimates of treatment effects in the presence of correlated errors from hierarchical data (Seltman, 2018). This is applicable to the present analyses because although there are a total of 1000 tokens, the data is clustered such that the data points come from four separate subjects. However, because LMEMs require that the dependent variable be normally distributed, it was not possible to explore for overall effects on the nominal categorical variables with more than two levels (i.e., pre-nuclear F0 rise pattern and BPM). The effect of utterance purpose and the presence of target items in the SDS speech style were also examined where relevant. Findings from within-subject and between-subject analyses were interpreted based on observations from previous research and the TAs' comments from the follow-up interviews.

To address the question of the influence of nativeness and professional training and experience, subgroups of NSTs (Lola and Alejandra) and NNSTs (Kate and Tammy) were created. A series of LMEMs were used first to look for trends in the groups separately for the effect of speech style, then another series of LMEMs explored the effect of nativeness on the SDS data alone. The same analyses were run on the conversational speech samples in order to establish a baseline for comparison. The main differences between NSTs and NNSTs discovered in the data were interpreted based on the previous quantitative analyses as well as the TAs' linguistic experiences with the TL, education and teacher training, and comments about their own teaching.

Finally, differences across time in SDS for the individual TAs were compared using chi-square tests of independence for categorical variables and least squares general linear models (GLMs) for continuous variables. GLMs are used to measure the linear relationship across more than two groups, in this case, time points. The variables identified as meaningful with regard to time in the semester in the within-subject analyses were also explored in between-subject analyses using LMEMs. The within-subject analyses were used to determine if time in the semester could be considered a statistically significant factor in the prosodic realizations by individual, whereas the between-subject analyses revealed how the TAs as a group modified their prosodic behavior throughout the semester. The findings were interpreted holistically alongside the results from previous analyses in order to provide precise descriptions of prosodic changes in SDS over time.

Notes

1 It is important to note here that naturally-occurring data has logistical downfalls that are minimized through methodological design, but some are unavoidable. For instance, due to the unscripted nature of speech, it is impossible to control for the presence of voiced consonants (e.g., [l]) and unvoiced consonants (e.g., [f]), and pitch lines are only visible when voicing occurs. For this reason, rises and falls in pitch are sometimes obscured in the data.
2 The use of human subjects was approved by the Institutional Review Board (IRB) under study ID number 2014–1388.
3 The low pitch register for all four participants was similar, so the pitch window was set as 75 Hz as the minimum value. Except for very extreme cases, Lola and Kate's ceiling was around 400 Hz, so their pitch maximum was set at 500 Hz. Alejandra and Tammy's ceiling was higher than the others, so their pitch maximum was set at 600 Hz.
4 The identities of all research participants are protected under pseudonyms.
5 Waiting two years after the original data collection to administer the follow-up interviews had several advantages. First, the data had already been analyzed which allowed the researcher to ask questions that specifically targeted the main prosodic trends from the first phase of data analysis. Second, Lola and Alejandra were teaching the course for the first time and were new to the university at the time of the SDS recording. They had both taught the class subsequent times between the class recordings and the follow-up interviews and had spent two more years on campus. Therefore, they were able to comment specifically on the influence of familiarity with the course of instruction and student body on their teaching.
6 The 350 ms pause threshold was designated according to native speaker perceptions of pause length as well as pause analyses of the data samples used for this research. The native speaker raters in Rao's (2010) judged a pause greater than 400 ms as a 'long pause' and a pause less than 400 ms as a 'short pause.' However, in the present investigation using spontaneous speech, a slightly shorter pause threshold was necessary to minimize the interference of background noise, thus more reliably capturing the measurements of F0 range, F0 mean, articulation rate, and mean intensity.

7 A common threshold for denoting an F0 rise or fall is a change of at least 7 Hz (Rao, 2009).

References

Árva, V., & Medgyes, P. (2000). Native and non-native teachers in the classroom. *ScienceDirect, 28*(3), 355–372. doi: 10.1016/S0346-251X(00)00017-8

Biersack, S., Kempe, V., & Knapton, L. (2005). Fine-tuning speech registers: A comparison of the prosodic features of child-directed and foreigner-directed speech. *Interspeech*, 2401–2404. doi: 10.13140/2.1.2133.5049

Blitt, M., Casas, M., & Copple, M. (2013). *Exploraciones: Curso intermedio*. Boston, MA: Cengage Learning.

Boersma, P., & Weenink, D. (2016). *Praat: Doing phonetics by computer [computer program]*, Version 6.0.19. Retrieved from www.praat.org/

Callahan, L. (2006). Student perceptions of native and non-native speaker language instructors: A comparison of ESL and Spanish. *Sintagma, 18*, 19–49. Retrieved from www.sintagma.udl.cat/en/

Canagarajah, S. (1999). Interrogating the "native-speaker fallacy": Non-linguistic roots, non-pedagogical results. In G. Braine (Ed.), *Non-native educators in English language teaching* (pp. 77–92). Mahwah, NJ: Lawrence Erlbaum. doi: 10.4324/9781315045368

Charness, G., Gneezy, U., & Kuhn, M. A. (2011). Experimental methods: Between-subject and within-subject design. *Journal of Economic Behavior & Organization, 81*, 1–8. doi: 10.1016/j.jebo.2011.08.009

Christie, F. (2002). *Classroom discourse analysis: A functional perspective*. London: Bloomsbury Publishing. doi: 10.1590/S0102-44502006000100012

Chun, D. M. (2002). *Discourse intonation in L2: From theory and research to practice*. Philadelphia, PA: John Benjamins. doi: 10.1075/lllt.1

Cook, V. (1999). Going beyond the native speaker in language teaching. *TESOL Quarterly, 33*(2), 185–209. doi: 10.2307/3587717

Cook, V. (2016). Where is the native speaker now? *TESOL Quarterly, 50*(1). doi: 10.1002/tesq.286

Ernestus, M., & Warner, N. (2011). An introduction to reduced pronunciation variants. *Journal of Phonetics*, 253–260. doi: 10.1016/S0095-4470(11)00055-6

Estebas Vilaplana, E., & Prieto, P. (2008). La notación prosódica en español. Une revisión del Sp_ToBI. *Estudios de Fonética Experimental, 17*, 263–283.

Face, T. L. (2001). *Intonational marking of contrastive focus in Madrid Spanish*, Ph. D. Dissertation. The Ohio State University.

Face, T. L. (2003). Intonation in Spanish declaratives: Difference between lab speech and spontaneous speech. *Catalan Journal of Linguistics*, 115–131. Retreived from https://revistes.uab.cat/catJL

Faraco, M., Kida, T., Barbier, M. L., & Piolat, A. (2002). Didactic prosody and notetaking in L1 and L2. In *Speech Prosody 2002, International Conference*.

Gerard, C., & Dahan, D. (1995). Durational variations in speech and didactic accent during reading. *Speech Communication, 16*(3), 293–311. doi: 10.1016/0167-6393(94)00060-N

Giles, H., & Coupland, N. (1991). *Language: Contexts and consequences*. Milton Keynes: Open University Press.

Golinkoff, R. M., Can, D. D., Soderstrom, M., & Hirsh-Pasek, K. (2015). (Baby) talk to me: The social context of infant-directed speech and its effects on early language acquisition. *Association for Psychological Science, 24*(5), 339–344. doi: 10.1177/0963721415595345

Gussenhoven, C. (2002). Intonation and interpretation: Phonetics and phonology. In *Speech Prosody 2002, International Conference*. Retrieved from https://perso.limsi.fr/mareuil/control/gussenhoven.pdf

Gut, U., Trouvain, J., & Barry, W. J. (2007). Bridging research on phonetic descriptions with knowledge from teaching practice: The case of prosody in non-native speech. In J. Trouvain, & U. Gut (Eds.), *Non-native prosody, phonetic description and teaching practice* (pp. 3–25). Berlin: Mouton de Gruyter. doi: 10.1515/9783110198751.0.3

Harding, J. (2013). *Qualitative data analysis from start to finish*. London: Sage.

Hertel, T., & Sunderman, G. (2009). Student attitudes toward native and non-native language instructors. *Foreign Language Annals, 42*, 468–482. doi: 10.1111/j.1944-9720.2009.01031.x

Hirst, D. J. (2006). Prosodic aspects of speech and language. In K. Brown, A. H. Anderson, M. Berns, G. Hirst, & J. Miller (Eds.), *Encyclopedia of language and linguistics* (2 ed., Vol. 10, pp. 167–178). Amsterdam and London: Elsevier. doi: 10.1016/B0-08-044854-2/00019-5

Hualde, J. I. (2007). Stress removal and stress addition in Spanish. *Journal of Portuguese Linguistics*, 59–89. doi: 10.5334/jpl.145

Inoue, F. (2006). Sociolinguistic characteristics of intonation. In Y. Kawaguchi, I. Fonágy, & T. Moriguchi (Eds.), *Prosody and syntax: Cross-linguistic perspectives* (pp. 197–223). Philadelphia, PA: John Benjamins. doi: 10.1075/ubli.3.12ino

Kuhl, P. K., Andruski, J. E., Chistovich, I. A., Chistovich, L. A., Kozhevnikova, E. V., Ryskina, V. L., Stolyarova, E. I., Sundberg, U., & Lacerda, F. (1997). Cross-language analysis of phonetic units in language addressed to infants. *Science, 277*(5326), 684–686. doi: 10.1126/science.277.5326.684

Labov, W. (1972). *Sociolinguistic patterns*. Philadelphia, PA: University of Pennsylvania Press.

Llurda, E. (2014). Non-native teachers and advocacy. In M. Bigelow, & J. Ennser-Kananen (Eds.), *The Routledge handbook of educational linguistics*, 105–116. doi: 10.4324/9781315797748

Medgyes, P. (1994). *The non-native teacher*. London: Macmillan.

Moussu, L., & Llurda, E. (2008). Non-native English-speaking English language teachers: History and research. *Language Teaching, 41*, 315–348. doi: 10.1017/S0261444808005028

Ohala, J. J. (1984). An ethological perspective on common cross-language utilization of F0 of voice. *Phonetica, 41*, 1–16. doi: 10.1159/000261706

O'Rourke, E. (2012). The realization of contrastive focus in Peruvian Spanish intonation. *Lingua, 494*–510. doi: 10.1016/j.lingua.2011.10.002

Payne, E., Post, B., Astruc, L., Prieto, P., & Vanrell, M. (2009). Rhythmic modification in child directed speech. *Oxford University Working Papers in Linguistics*,

Philology & Phonetics, 123–144. Retrieved from www.ling-phil.ox.ac.uk/files/uploads/OWP2009.pdf

Prieto, P. (2006). Phonological phrasing in Spanish. In S. Colina, & F. Martínez (Eds.), *Optimality-theoretic advances in Spanish phonology* (pp. 39–60). Amsterdam/Philadelphia: John Benjamins. doi: 10.1075/la.99.03pri

Rao, R. (2006). On intonation's relationship with pragmatic meaning in Spanish. *Proceedings of the 8th Hipanic Linguistics Symposium* (pp. 103–115). Somerville, MA: Cascadilla Press.

Rao, R. (2009). Deaccenting in spontaneous speech in Barcelona Spanish. *Studies in Hispanic and Lusophone Linguistics, 2*(1), 31–75. doi: 10.1515/shll-2009-1035

Rao, R. (2010). Final lengthening and pause duration in three dialects of Spanish. In M. Ortega-Llebaria (Ed.), *Selected Proceedings of the 4th Conference on Laboratory Approaches to Spanish Phonology* (pp. 69–82). Somerville, MA: Cascadilla Proceedings Project.

Rao, R. (2011). Intonation in Spanish classroom-style didactic speech. *Journal of Teaching and Research, 3*, 31–75. doi: 10.4304/jltr.2.3.493-507

Samimy, R., & Brutt-Griffler, J. (1999). To be a native or non-native speaker: Perceptions of "nonnative" students in a graduate TESOL program. In G. Braine (Ed.), *Nonnative educators in English language teaching* (pp. 127–144). Mahwah, NJ: Lawrence Erlbaum. doi: 10.4324/9781315045368

Scarborough, R., Brenier, J., Zhao, Y., Hall-Lew, L., & Dmitrieva, O. (2007). An acoustic study of real and imagined foreigner-directed speech. In J. Trouvain, & W. J. Barry (Ed.), *Proceedings of the 16th International Conference of the Phonetic Sciences* (pp. 2165–2168). Saarbruecken, Germany. doi: 10.1121/1.4781735

Schilling, N. (2013). Investigating stylistic variation. In J. K. Chambers, & N. Schilling (Eds.), *The handbook of language variation and change* (2nd ed., pp. 325–349). Hoboken, NJ: Wiley-Blackwell. doi: 10.1002/9781118335598.ch15

Seltman, H. J. (2018). *Experimental design and analysis*. Unpublished manuscript, Carnegie Mellon University, Pittsburgh, PA. Retrieved from www.stat.cmu.edu/~hseltman/309/Book/Book.pdf

Stanley, P., & Stevenson, M. (2017). Making sense of not making sense: Novice English language teacher talk. *Linguistics and Education*, 1–10. doi: 10.1016/j.linged.2017.01.001

Tobin, K., King, D., Henderson, S., Bellocchi, A., & Ritchie, S. M. (2016). Expression of emotions and physiological change during teaching. *Cultural Studies of Science Education, 11*, 669–692. doi: 10.1007/s11422-016-9778-9

Torres Cacoullos, R., & Travis, C. E. (2013). Gauging convergence on the ground: Code-switching in the community. *International Journal of Bilingualism*, 1–21. doi: 10.1177/1367006913516046

Üstünel, E., & Seedhouse, P. (2005). Why that, in that language, right now? Code-switching and pedagogical focus. *International Journal of Applied Linguistics, 15*(3), 302–325. doi: 10.1111/j.1473-4192.2005.00093.x

Uther, M., Knoll, M. A., & Burnham, D. (2007). Do you speak E-NG-L-I-SH? A comparison of foreigner- and infant-directed speech. *Speech Communication*, 2–7. doi: 10.1016/j.specom.2006.10.003

Walsh, S. (2013). *Classroom discourse and teacher development.* Edinburgh: Edinburgh University Press. doi: 10.3366/j.ctt1g0b484.6

Willis, J. (1992). Inner and outer: Spoken discourse in the language classroom. In M. Coulthard (Ed.), *Advances in spoken discourse analysis* (pp. 162–182). London: Routledge. doi: 10.4324/9780203200063

5 Prosodic correlates of SDS

Introduction

To identify prosodic features of SDS as it occurs in intermediate L2 Spanish classrooms, descriptive and statistical analyses of prosodic features are presented here along with biographical and observation-based evidence from the data. Within- and between-subject statistical analyses reveal whether differences in SDS and conversational speech can be attributed to chance alone. Differences between the speech styles regarding articulation rate, intensity, F0 mean, F0 range, F0 pre-nuclear rise pattern, and BPM were statistically significant for the majority of the participants. Other prosodic features such as F0 peak frequency were significantly different between speech styles for some participants but not others. For each measure, raw and statistical data are presented, and findings are interpreted based on the biographical background, education, training, and experience of the TAs, their personal comments generated during the follow-up interviews, and evidence from previous research on speech prosody. By looking at prosodic trends from numerous perspectives, we gain a more comprehensive understanding of SDS as it occurs in the L2 classroom.

Articulation rate and intensity

Results

Overall, the TAs utilized slower speech rate and higher average intensity during SDS when compared to conversational speech. Figure 5.1 displays overlaid intensity contours from utterances produced by Lola. The SDS utterance "*si pienso que está bien os pondré la nota y si no igual lo cambio un poco*" 'if I think it's ok, I will give you the grade and if not I will change it a little' is drawn with a solid line, and the utterance from conversational speech "*yo tampoco sé cómo integrar y cómo relacionarlo porque*

Prosodic correlates of SDS 67

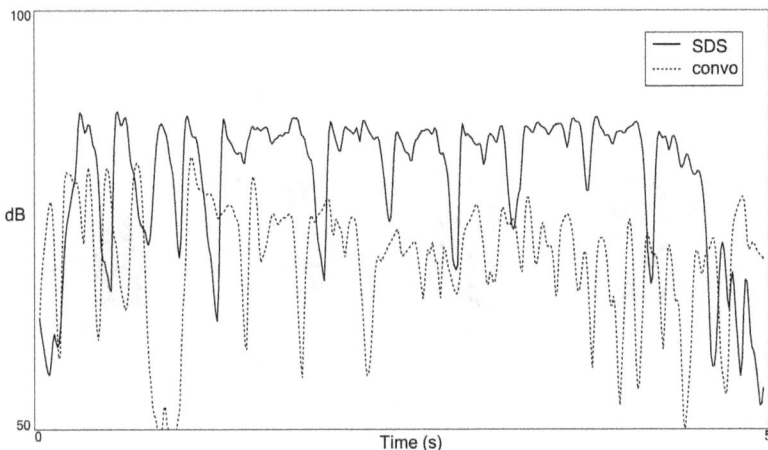

Figure 5.1 Intensity contours in SDS and conversation.

se supone que si la pones en clase tienes que contextualizarlo" 'I also don't know how to integrate and how to connect it because supposedly if you put it up in class, then you have to contextualize it' is drawn with a dashed line. The average intensity of the SDS utterance is 83.46 dB, while the average intensity of the conversational utterance is 73.88 dB, a difference of nearly 10 dB. This pattern of increased intensity in SDS is common in the data of all participants. Additionally, both utterances are five seconds in duration, but the SDS phrase contains 21 syllables and the conversational speech phrase contains 41 syllables. This drastic decrease in speech rate is seen throughout Lola's SDS.

Three out of four participants used a slower rate of articulation during SDS when compared to conversational speech; only Kate spoke more slowly during conversational speech. Figure 5.2 displays the average articulation rates for each participant in each speech style. Lola and Alejandra spoke more rapidly in conversational speech than in SDS by 10 or more sylls/s on average. Tammy's articulation rate varied on average by only 0.4 sylls/s between speech styles, and Kate spoke more quickly during SDS by an average of 0.3 sylls/s. Independent sample *t*-tests revealed statistical significance[1] for the difference in articulation rate across speech styles for all three TAs who spoke more swiftly during conversational speech than SDS,[2] indicated in Figure 5.2 by asterisks after the names of the TAs on the horizontal axis.[3] The difference in articulation rate by speech style was not significant for Kate.[4] Additionally, despite the significant differences in speech rate

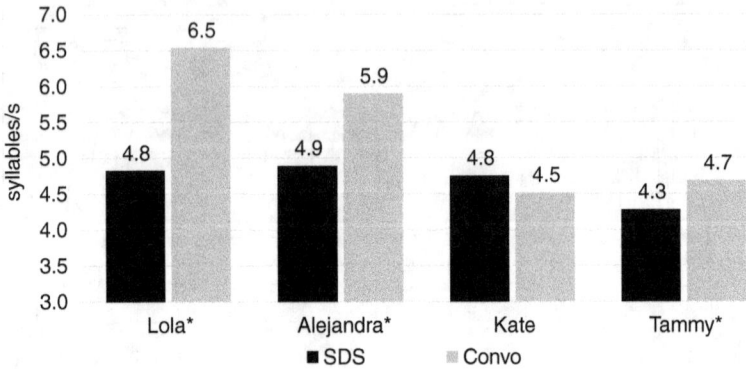

Figure 5.2 Articulation rate in SDS and conversation.

across speech style for the three TAs, the between-subject statistical tests using LMEMs[5] revealed that this difference by speech style was not significant for the participants as a group.[6]

In addition to differences in articulation rate, all four TAs used greater intensity levels during SDS than conversational speech by a margin of 2 to 4 dBs on average. Figure 5.3 displays the average intensity used by each participant in both speech styles. The differences by speech style for mean intensity were determined to be statistically significant for all participants through independent sample t-tests.[7] Additionally, intensity in SDS overall

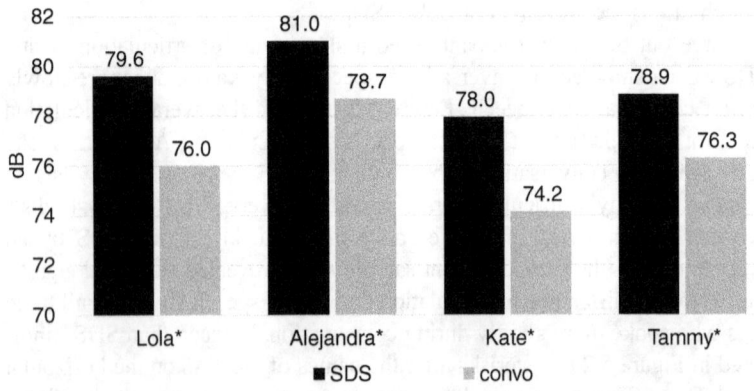

Figure 5.3 Mean intensity in SDS and conversation.*

was found to be significantly higher than in conversational speech according to a LMEM.[8]

Discussion

It was expected that the TAs would speak more slowly with students based on previous research on teacher talk, didactic speech in general, and similar speech styles such as IDS and FDS. Even though articulation rate was a significant factor differentiating the speech styles for three of the four TAs in the data, Kate actually spoke more swiftly during SDS. In the follow-up interviews when Kate was asked about how she speaks differently in the classroom than to a friend or colleague, she claimed that she tries to speak in a natural way to her students. Unprompted to talk specifically about speech rate, she responded, "Speaking not even necessarily always slower because they need to have a challenge to not, you know, have everything separated or enunciated." Kate's perspective helps clarify the findings here. She may have been dedicating so much effort to sounding natural for her students that she actually surpassed her more natural speech rate according to the conversational speech data used for comparison. Additionally, Kate mentioned several times in the interview that the class she had the semester of the data collection was frustrating and stressful because the location was far from the center of campus, so the students often arrived late. She often had to assign other activities in the beginning of class to allow time for the students to trickle in, then did not have time to cover the course material during the rest of class. This is a logical explanation for Kate's quickened speech rate during SDS.

So, although there are many reasons to believe that teacher talk involves slower speech, there are situations in which swifter speech is used in the classroom depending on the instructor, students, or discourse situation. In the follow-up interviews, Tammy commented that she reads true or false statements (common in activities used for classwork, homework, and assessments) aloud to her students at a moderate pace, not too quickly or too slowly, to ensure that they understand, but also to not sound unnatural. She also said that she slows down her speech when giving instructions, but if she's reading a dialogue or something similar (which she uses to model the TL to her students), she will speed up. Additionally, Tammy slows her speech in order to emphasize verbs that let the students know what they are supposed to be doing at a particular moment. Similarly, Lola asserted that in general she speaks much more slowly when addressing students than when speaking with friends or colleagues, and if something is important to the class, she will speak even more slowly and clearly so that her students understand her. Alejandra also said that she slows down when addressing students, but that she sometimes forgets and speaks quickly. However, Alejandra was very surprised with how slowly she was speaking when she heard a clip of herself giving instructions during the second recorded class, and said that perhaps it had to do with the fact that she was giving instructions at that moment, and that she typically spends more time on giving instructions than other functions during class. All these assertions from the TAs support the conclusion that while SDS typically involves a slower speech rate, variation should be expected.

Intensity was found to be a significant factor distinguishing speech style in both the within-subject analyses for each TA and the between-subject analysis. This is not surprising given that SDS involves a presentational speech setting where the presenter, in this case the TAs, must speak louder to be heard. The language differential between the teachers and students also explains the significant findings for intensity during SDS, as proficient language users tend to speak louder when addressing those with more limited proficiency, as discussed in Chapter 3 in the section on FDS. Intensity is strengthened in formal and accommodative speech styles that involve careful, monitored articulation. In the follow-up interviews, Lola said that she tries to be clearer and more precise in class so that the students can understand her, and the other TAs made similar assertions. What's more, intensity is involved in portraying acoustic prominence involved in emphasis contexts. All four TAs talked about how they emphasize and exaggerate their speech when addressing students. Tammy said that students at the intermediate level are still new with regard to exposure to the TL and, therefore, benefit from the use of clear, direct, and exaggerated speech. In summary, increased intensity during SDS can be largely attributed to vocal projection, clarity, and emphasis.

Pitch mean and range

Results

Across the data, the TAs produced utterances with higher average F0 and wider F0 range in SDS when compared to conversational speech. These overall trends by speech style are apparent in the pitch contours throughout the data. For instance, Figure 5.4 displays pitch tracks from two utterances of similar length and articulation rate (about 600 ms at 4.4 sylls/s), one from SDS on the first recording day drawn with a solid line and one from conversational speech drawn with a dashed line, both produced by Tammy. The SDS utterance *"tenemos más o menos media hora y lo que tengo aquí para ustedes es un repaso"* 'we have about half an hour and what I have here for you is a review' contains two minor *ips* within the

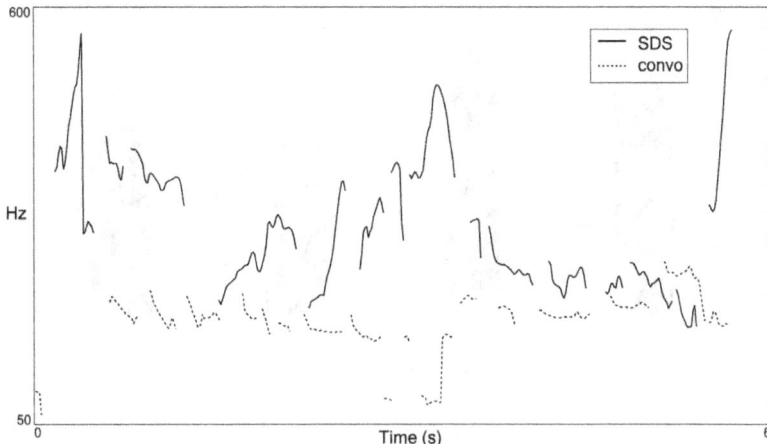

Figure 5.4 Pitch contours in SDS and conversation.

superior IP, each bound with high initial tones, rising and high-rising boundary tones, and downstepped pre-nuclear peaks. The average F0 mean in the utterance is 318 Hz, with a F0 range of 556 Hz. For comparison, the conversational speech utterance "*y que todos nosotros tenemos niveles diferentes de esta creencia*" 'and that we all have different levels of this belief,' was produced in a considerably lower pitch register (mean of 189 Hz) and using a much narrower pitch range (194 Hz). It contained one IP ending with falling boundary movement following an upstepped nuclear F0 peak.

Overall, the TAs used an average F0 mean of 252 Hz during SDS compared to 197 Hz in conversational speech. Figure 5.5 shows the average F0 means in each speech type for the TAs individually. Independent *t*-tests comparing the within-subject means revealed that the differences in F0 mean according to speech style were statistically significant for all TAs.[9] Additionally, the between-subject analysis using a LMEM revealed that F0 mean was significantly higher in SDS than in conversational speech in the data overall.[10]

With regard to F0 range, the TAs produced wider F0 range values on average in SDS (232.6 Hz) when compared to conversational speech (173.2 Hz). Figure 5.6 shows the average F0 range employed by each TA in SDS compared to conversational speech. All participants used a wider pitch range in SDS, but according to the results of independent *t*-tests, the difference in F0 range across speech styles was only significant for Lola,[11]

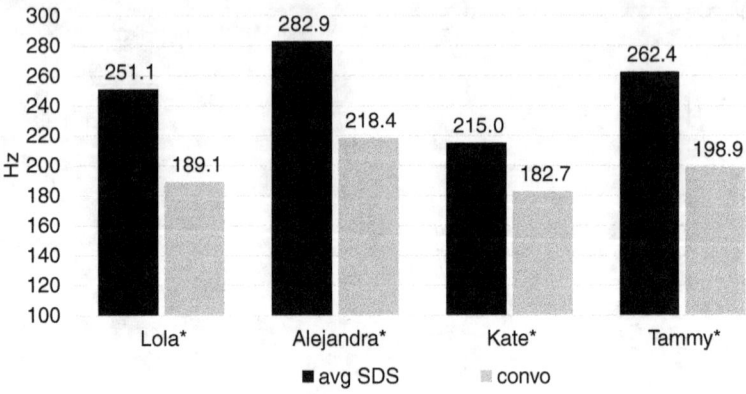

Figure 5.5 F0 mean in SDS and conversation.*

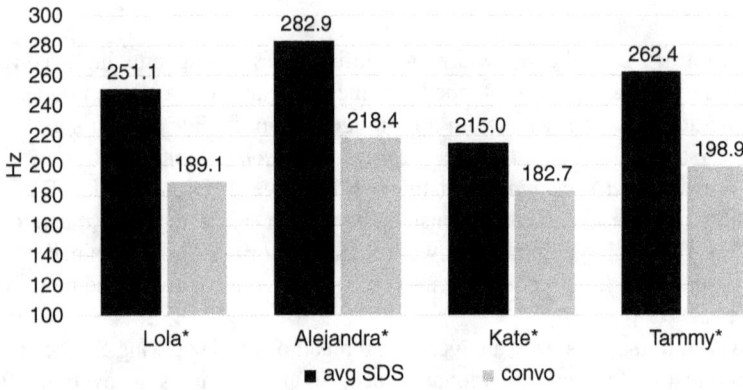

Figure 5.6 F0 range in SDS and conversation.*

Alejandra,[12] and Tammy,[13] to the exclusion of Kate.[14] In the between-subject analysis, results of the LMEM revealed that F0 range was significantly wider in SDS than in conversational speech across all participants.[15]

Discussion

Pitch mean was found to be statistically significant in both the within- and between-subject analyses, but while pitch range was significant in the between-subject analysis, it was not found to be statistically significant in the within-subject analysis of Kate's speech. Although she used a wider F0 range on average in SDS compared to conversational speech, the difference for Kate was less extreme than for the other TAs. Kate varied pitch by an average of 175 Hz in her SDS phrases while the other TAs all produced an average pitch range of more than 214 Hz. An explanation for the lack of significance in Kate's samples was discovered in the follow-up interview when, unprompted to talk about pitch or tone, Kate commented that she tries to portray a sense of calm and confidence while speaking to a class by using an even tone as opposed to a H tone. She also tries to be serious and direct in order to gain an authoritative presence. These assertions help explain why the difference between F0 range in SDS and conversational speech is less extreme for Kate compared to the other TAs, all of whom stressed that they wanted their students to feel comfortable and at ease.

Additionally, it is important to point out that there was considerable variation across the TAs with regard to pitch range. Tammy varied between speech styles the most (by an average of 104 Hz) followed by Lola who varied by an average of 69 Hz. Despite interparticipant variation, the higher pitch registers and wider F0 ranges employed during SDS by the TAs can be explained in several ways. According to Gussenhoven's (2002) biological codes, H tones can be associated with the speakers' desire to capture the listeners' attention, which is one of the functions of SDS discussed previously. Increased F0 height (and, consequently, F0 mean) as an attention-getting mechanism has been reported in studies on IDS, qualitative studies on teacher talk, and experimental studies on didactic speech. Therefore, it is possible that, given that the TAs are in charge in the classroom, they are employing a higher pitch register and wider range in SDS to engage students and hold their attention. Verifying this hypothesis, Tammy claimed in her follow-up interview that she used higher tones in the classroom similar to "baby babble" to engage her listeners. She compared the H tone of her SDS with the way she speaks to her baby son. Alejandra mentioned that she tries to use *"un tono no aburrido"* 'a tone that is not boring' when speaking to the students as a group in her classroom in order to hold their attention.

The significantly higher F0 mean and wider F0 range employed during SDS can also be explained by pragmatic and communicative functions involved in classroom discourse. As discussed in Chapter 1, H tones and wide F0 ranges are often associated with friendliness, gentleness, or kindness. During the follow-up interviews, Lola, Alejandra, and Tammy all talked about how they want their students to feel comfortable in class, so they try to portray themselves as kind and approachable. Alejandra even asserted that she believes that she comes across as more friendly when she speaks with a higher tone, and that she consciously uses a higher pitch register to portray this attitude to her students. Both Lola and Alejandra stressed the importance of making students feel comfortable so that they volunteer more often during class and speak more with their classmates during interactive activities. Additionally, all four TAs talked about how they emphasize important content and TL items during classroom speech. Marking salience of target or communicatively important items manifests itself as an increase in pitch mean and a widening of pitch range, so these functions explain the significant findings in this research.

F0 peak frequency and pre-nuclear F0 rise pattern

Results

Along with F0 mean and range, an analysis of F0 contour shape reveals more fine-grained details about SDS prosody and how it diverges from conversational speech. The phrases extracted from the SDS samples on the whole consist of shorter, choppier phrases that are riddled with frequent pauses, features that have been observed in other research on language grading and the didactic speech style. The average phrase length in SDS does not exceed 2.5 seconds for any TA, while the average length of conversational phrases is equal to or greater than 2.5 seconds for all TAs. In addition to longer phrases, the TAs produced more lexically stressed words per second in conversational speech than SDS, with the exception of Kate who produced more stressed words per second in SDS than conversational speech. Lexically stressed words in this measurement are not necessarily accompanied by F0 movement. Due to increased phrasal segmentation in SDS, phrases typically consisted of fewer lexically stressed words.

It was very uncommon for F0 peaks to be suppressed in SDS where they are often suppressed in conversation, and phrases containing more than six F0 peaks were relatively infrequent in SDS. Contrastingly, it was found in the data that conversational speech involved more instances of F0 suppression as well as the opposite extreme, rapid F0 movement, and fewer cases of phrases with one to three peaks when compared to SDS. Figure 5.7 represents the utterance "*lo que es importante es que con indicativo son cosas que existen*" 'what is important is that with indicative they are things that exist' produced by Lola in SDS, and Figure 5.8 represents the utterance "*veinte años máximo cuando salen van a volver a hacerlo porque esa gente no se recupera bueno está comprobado porque los que salieron de ...*" 'twenty years maximum when they get out they are going to do it again because those people do not recover well this has been proven because those that got

Prosodic correlates of SDS 75

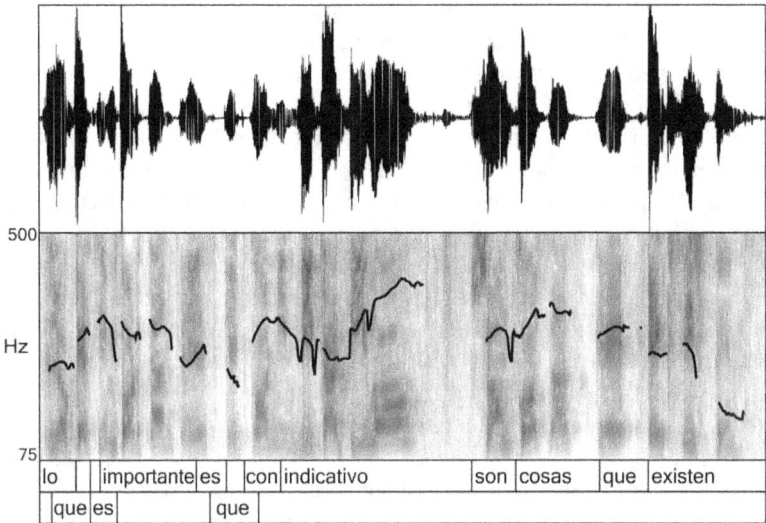

Figure 5.7 Pitch contour in SDS.

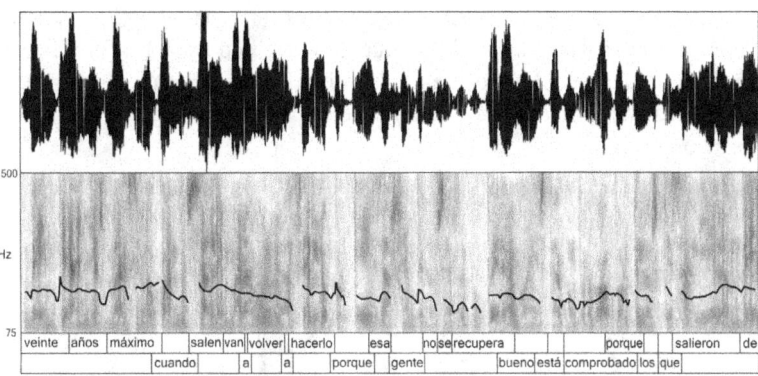

Figure 5.8 Pitch contour in conversation.

out of ...' from Lola's conversational speech. Both utterances are approximately six seconds in duration. Pauses can be identified by breaks in the wavelengths in the top portion of each figure, breaks in the pitch tracks traced in black, and the absence of voicing (seen through whitening in the spectrogram). Comparing the utterances, we see that Lola utilized shorter phrases in SDS with less suppression of medial peaks.

76 Prosodic correlates of SDS

Phrases containing one to three F0 peaks were the most common trend in both SDS and conversational speech data, but they were relatively more frequent in SDS. However, as evidenced in the data, the measurement of F0 peak frequency was influenced by the short phrasal segmentation in SDS, so F0 peak frequency per second was calculated as a more representative measure of the frequency of occurrence of F0 peaks throughout phrases in the two speech styles. Three of the four participants utilized a greater frequency of F0 peaks per second in SDS than conversational speech, but Alejandra's speech styles exhibited almost identical F0 peak frequency and Tammy actually utilized a greater number of F0 peaks on average in conversational speech. Figure 5.9 shows the average number of F0 peaks uttered per second by the participants in SDS and conversational speech. The difference in F0 peak frequency by speech style was statistically significant for Lola[16] and Kate[17] according to a series of independent *t*-tests. Statistical tests for the effect of speech style on F0 peak frequency were not significant for Alejandra nor Tammy.[18] In the between-subject analysis, the LMEM revealed that F0 peak frequency was a significant factor for speech style across the data of the participants.[19]

Based on the separate analysis of pre-nuclear F0 peak patterns, more than 50% of the contours measured in conversational speech for each participant were categorized as downstepped. In SDS, the frequency of downstepped phrases dropped to below 40% for Lola and Alejandra and below 50% for Kate, while the frequency increased by 4.3% for Tammy, corresponding with slight decreases in other F0 rise patterns such as those associated with narrow focus, erratic peaks, and hyper regular peaks. For

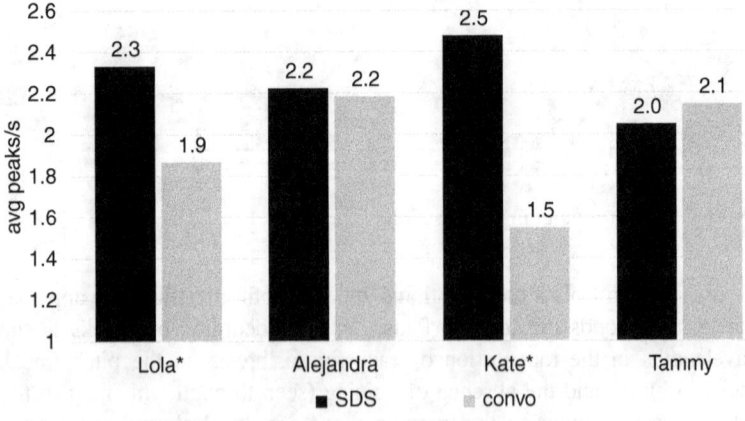

Figure 5.9 F0 peaks per second in SDS and conversation.*

the other three TAs, pre-nuclear F0 rise patterns other than downstepping remained more or less stable across speech styles with the exception of the category denoting the absence of a pattern, which included phonetically reduced phrases and those that were too short in length (or too riddled with pauses) to involve F0 movement. The percent of phrases lacking F0 rise patterns increased for all four participants in SDS compared to conversational speech. These trends are visualized in Figures 5.7 and 5.8, presented previously from Lola's speech samples. The high frequency of pauses in the SDS utterance prevents the formation of expected pre-nuclear F0 rise patterning observed in the conversational speech utterance exhibiting a series of downstepped contours and hyper regular F0 peaks. A chi-square test of independence[20] showed that the difference in pre-nuclear F0 rise patterns across speech style was statistically significant for Lola,[21] Alejandra,[22] and Kate,[23] but not for Tammy.[24]

Discussion

While all TAs produced shorter phrases in SDS compared to conversational speech, the difference was more extreme for Lola and Kate. Lola produced a proportionate amount of lexically stressed words across speech styles, but Kate did not. In fact, Kate produced more stressed words per second in SDS despite using shorter phrases. This corresponds with Kate's faster articulation rate during SDS compared to conversation. While she uttered long phrases with relatively few breaks and intonational phrase boundaries during conversational speech, she spoke slower and produced fewer lexically stressed words per second than the other TAs. However, in SDS, her rate of articulation, length of phrases, and frequency of lexically stressed words uttered per second were comparable to the other TAs. While it is interesting that Kate diverged from her peers in the conversational setting, her prosodic behaviors in the classroom were similar.

Increased phrasal segmentation and slower articulation rate during SDS have several secondary effects on the shape of F0 contours. First, there were more phrases containing one to three F0 peaks in SDS than conversational speech but fewer instances of complete F0 suppression and phrases containing more than three F0 peaks. The relative infrequency of phrases containing more than three peaks can be attributed to the shorter phrases in SDS. F0 suppression, on the other hand, merits closer examination. The measure of F0 peak frequency per second revealed that two of the TAs produced significantly more F0 peaks per second in SDS compared to conversational speech, and an overall trend between participants was also corroborated through statistical evidence. This utterance-medial F0 strengthening during SDS contrasts with studies on narrow focus expression that describe non-focal F0 peak suppression as a strategy used to attract more attention to the focused constituent. This was not found in the current investigation, possibly because of the rampant phrase segmentation occurring during SDS and overall phonetic strengthening phenomena involved in this speech style.

The presence of utterance-medial strengthening in SDS could be attributed to speech rate: F0 suppression is more common in quicker, less monitored speech styles such as conversational speech, which would explain why Lola and Kate suppress utterance-medial F0 peaks significantly more frequently during conversational speech. However, Kate used a faster speech rate as well as significantly more F0 peaks per second during SDS than conversational speech. Therefore, speech rate is not a suitable explanation for this finding. Another explanation for the higher frequency of F0 peaks per second in Lola and Kate's SDS could be personality. In the follow-up interviews, all the TAs made reference to how their personalities affect their teaching. Both Lola and Kate made comments alluding to the fact that they self-identify as introverts, so they make efforts to be assertive and authoritative in class, while Alejandra and Tammy talked about how they are outgoing in general and with their students. It is possible that Lola and Kate's timid personalities came across as suppressed F0 peaks during conversational speech. A closer look at the findings show that both Lola and Kate produced fewer than 1.9 peaks per second in conversational speech, while Alejandra and Tammy produced more than 2.1 peaks per second in conversation. Therefore, we can conclude that Lola and Kate's efforts to lead the class resulted in a greater frequency of F0 peaks per second in SDS, thus yielding significant differences in peak frequency across speech styles for these TAs.

Results from the comparison of pre-nuclear F0 rise patterns in SDS and conversational speech also reflect the excess of short, choppy phrases in SDS consistent with research on language grading and the didactic speech style. There were fewer instances of typical broad focus declarative pre-nuclear F0 rise patterns in SDS when compared to conversational speech. While downstepping was by far the most common shape of utterances in conversational speech, many of the utterances in SDS were too short to contain multiple F0 peaks, so downstepping and other pre-nuclear peak patterns were less common. Phrases with standard pre-nuclear pitch migrations were relatively infrequent in SDS; however, from an impressionistic perspective, phrases were downstepped relative to one another in this speech style. For example, there was an overarching downstepping of phrases throughout instructional utterances that was obscured by frequent pauses, shorter phrase segmentation, and special emphasis contexts during SDS. This explains the results relating to pre-nuclear F0 rise patterns in this investigation.

Boundary pitch movement

Results

SDS speech contained more boundary movement overall. Across all participants, boundary tones were present in 61.6% of the SDS phrases and only 30.8% of the conversational phrases. Figure 5.10 shows the percentage of BPM types for all participants in both speech styles. "No BPM" represents phrases that did not exhibit F0 movement at the final boundary.

A visual example is provided in Figure 5.11 which represents a typical pitch contour from Kate's SDS speech sample on recording day 3. The

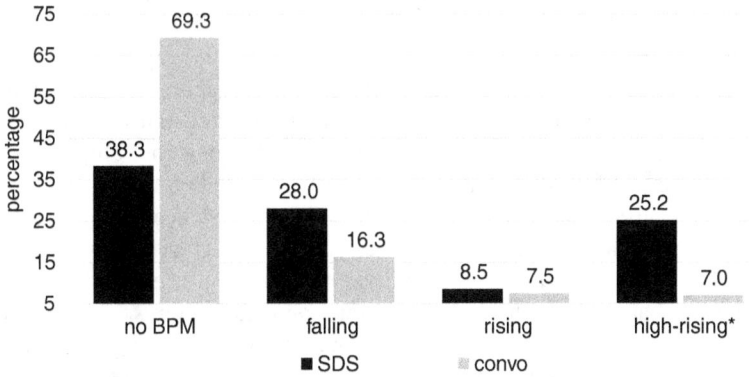

Figure 5.10 BPM frequency in SDS and conversation.

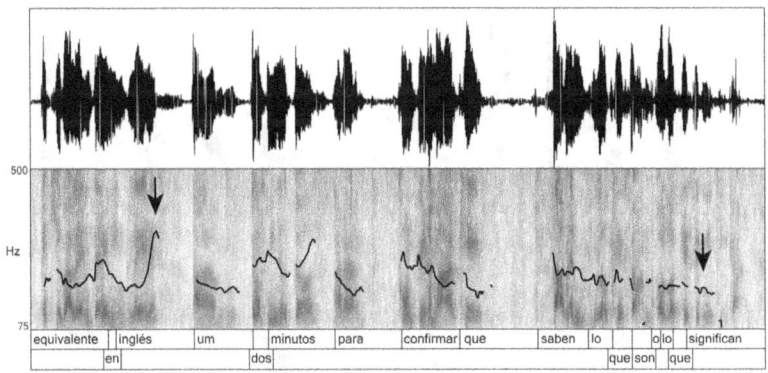

Figure 5.11 Pitch contour showing BPM in SDS and conversation.

utterance "*equivalente en inglés ... um ... dos minutos para ... confirmar que ... saben lo que son o lo que significan*" 'equivalent in English ... um ... two minutes to ... confirm that ... you know what they are or what they mean' contained high-rising boundary movement, indicated with the first black arrow, and falling boundary movement, indicated with the second black arrow.

Figure 5.12 shows the percentage of BPM types present in each participants' SDS. All four TAs produced more falling and high-rising contours in SDS than in conversational speech. As for rising contours, Lola and Kate used more rising contours in SDS when compared to conversational speech, while Alejandra and Tammy produced fewer in SDS than in conversation. Chi-square tests looking at the frequency of falling, rising, and high-rising BPM for the TAs individually revealed statistically significant differences in BPM across speech styles for Lola,[25] Alejandra,[26] and Tammy,[27] but not Kate.[28]

Additionally, compared to conversational speech, high-rising boundary movement seemed to be the behavior triggered most by the SDS speech style given the largest degree of change across all participants, followed by falling boundary movement. For this reason, within-subject analyses using chi-square tests of independence were used to determine if there was an effect of speech style on high-rising and falling BPM styles in isolation for each individual TA. Results revealed statistical significance for high-rising BPM for Lola and Tammy,[29] but not for Alejandra or Kate.[30] For the effect of speech style on falling BPM, the results of chi-square tests were not significant.[31] Between-subject

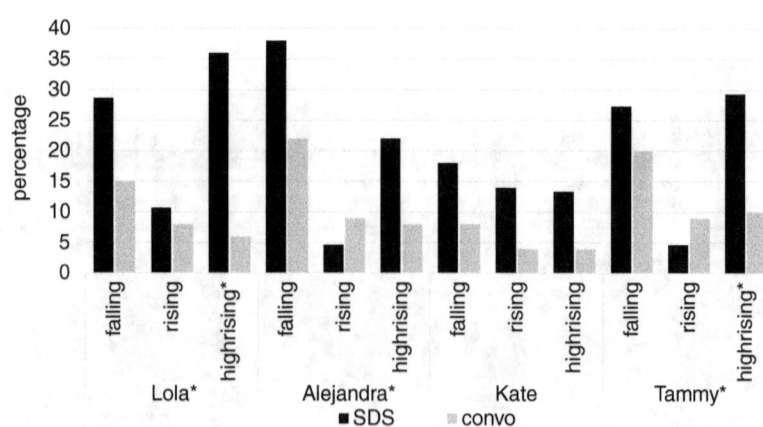

Figure 5.12 BPM shapes in SDS and conversation.

analyses using LMEMs were also utilized to test for the effect of speech style on the presence of high-rising and falling boundary tones. The models confirmed that final high-rises were significantly more frequent in SDS than in conversational speech across all subjects.[32] Falling boundary tones, however, were not found to be statistically significant as an indicator of speech style across subjects.[33]

To take a closer look at the implementation of high-rising boundary tones during SDS, the frequency of BPM types in utterances grouped by function is explored. The general breakdown of utterances in SDS by purpose is displayed in Figure 5.13. The majority of the phrases analyzed were categorized as instructional or administrative, followed by those containing examples of target items or correct language forms. Less common utterances included those of repair or recast of a student error and read speech, in that order. Neutral utterances, such as salutations, jokes, asides, etc., were the least common types of phrases in the data.

In order to evaluate the effect of utterance purpose on BPM, it was necessary to merge the categories of neutral speech, read speech or activity prompt, and repair or recast of student response. A within-subject analysis was performed first for the TAs individually, then a between-subject analysis was used to see how purpose influences BPM. A chi-square test of independence revealed statistical significance for Alejandra,[34] but not the other three TAs.[35] Alejandra used final falling tones while modeling speech and during neutral speech, read speech, and repair, and she used high-rising boundary tones mostly while modeling the target language and giving

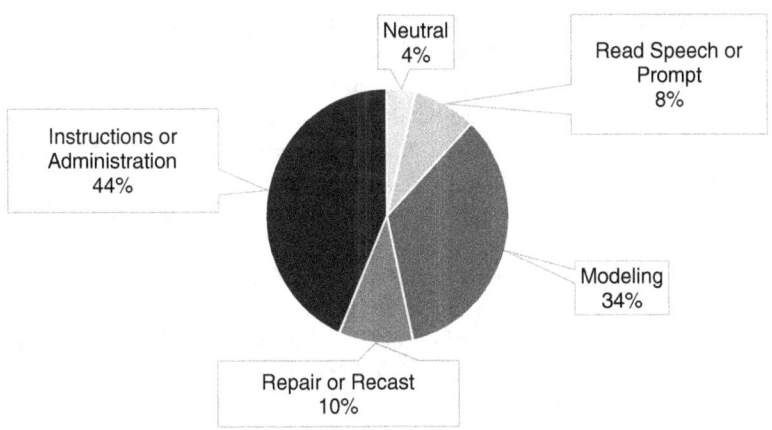

Figure 5.13 Utterance purpose in SDS.

instructions. Instructional phrases were rarely terminated with falling tones. Chi-square tests isolating falling boundary tones as they correlate with utterance purpose also revealed statistical significance in Alejandra's SDS speech,[36] but not for the other TAs.[37] The results of chi-square tests for the effect of utterance purpose on high-rising boundary tones in isolation were not significant for any of the TAs.[38]

Results from the LMEM[39] revealed that, across all participants, high-rising boundary tones in the SDS data as a whole were a statistically significant indicator of utterance purpose.[40] High-rising tones were not found to be associated statistically with phrases containing target language words or structures,[41] but were most common during instruction and administration. Falling boundary tones were not significantly correlated with utterance purpose[42] or the presence of target words or structures.[43]

Discussion

SDS was rich in phrase-final pitch movement, which coordinated with the higher frequency of shorter phrases in the speech style. Final falling and high-rising tones were more frequent in SDS for all four TAs, and rising boundary tones were more frequent in SDS for two TAs. Differences in BPM across speech styles were statistically significant for three of the TAs, but not for Kate. This finding is particularly interesting because, as mentioned previously, Kate produced significantly more F0 peaks per second in SDS when compared to conversational speech, so it would be expected that she would also use more pitch modulation at phrase boundaries. Taking a closer look at Figure 5.12, Kate did in fact produce about 10% more boundary tones in SDS than conversational speech, so while the difference was not extreme, BPM trends in Kate's speech were consistent with those of the other TAs and with other prosodic patterns observed in her SDS.

Looking at high-rising and falling BPM, both Lola and Tammy used significantly more high-rising boundary movement in SDS than conversational speech, but no significant differences between speech styles were discovered for falling boundary movement. A closer examination of BPM during SDS reveals when and why TAs used boundary tones, particularly the frequent falling and high-rising patterns. BPM was significantly associated with utterance purpose in Alejandra's SDS to the exclusion of the other TAs. In between-subject analyses, falling BPM was not significantly associated with utterance purpose across TAs in SDS while high-rising BPM was. As expected, high-rising BPM was most common during instruction or administration.

Alejandra utilized falling tones significantly more often when modeling correct speech and in neutral utterances, read speech, and repair and recast of student responses, and she hardly ever terminated instructional or administrative phrases with falling pitch contours. Instructional phrases were most often bound with high-rising F0 movement, which Alejandra herself claimed were used as rhetorical checks to ensure comprehension of important information imparted during instruction, although high-rises were not significantly associated with purpose in the individual within-subject test. Alejandra's utilization of phrase boundary cues to send messages to the learners can be explained by her teacher training or previous experience teaching languages.[44] She had taught L2 Spanish courses as well as L2 English and L2 French conversation courses previously, and Alejandra made mention in the follow-up interviews of the importance of using body language and tonal cues to portray information to the students. This has implications for teacher training and experience discussed in Chapter 7.

The significant findings with regard to high-rising BPM and speech style are particularly noteworthy as high-rising BPM has not been identified previously as a feature of didactic speech, to the knowledge of the researcher. As described previously, high-rising intonation has been tied to the expression of continuation or non-finality (i.e., to indicate that the speaker has not yet finished his or her talk turn), rhetorical questioning or utterances intended to seek confirmation or check for understanding, and affective messages such as friendliness and compassion. These functions are all relevant to the classroom setting and explain the prevalence of high-rising tones in SDS.

During the follow-up interviews, the TAs heard audio clips of themselves using high-rising final intonation during instructional talk. Alejandra said that until she heard the clip, she had not been aware of her use of high-rising boundary tones in SDS. She remembered trying to be "slow and nice," but did not intend to use high-rising BPM. She postulated that the high-rises were intended to give the students an opportunity to respond and show they were following her, or possibly to make them feel more comfortable or included. This was echoed by Tammy, who explained high-rising phrase boundaries in her SDS as a response-seeking mechanism. Tammy was also surprised by her own high-rising intonation. In the beginning of the follow-up interviews, she claimed that she was concerned with whether her students were interpreting her utterances as statements or questions; however, after hearing a clip of herself reading true or false statements, she realized that the frequent high-rises obscured the portrayal of sentence type through phrase final cues. Tammy said, "I was inflecting at the end or going up which I don't think it was a question." When prompted as to why she was inflecting in such a way, she described it as a cue to indicate to students that was their turn to talk or respond in some way.

Lola was aware of her final high-rising tendencies in SDS before the follow-up interview but claimed that she was not aware of her habit at the time of the data collection. She had become more aware of it as she had more experience teaching. After hearing a clip from her SDS that contained final high-rising intonation, she claimed that she was using high-rising boundary tones to hold the student's attention and emphasize important items. After further questioning, Lola went on to say that the intonational patterns could also be transfer from English, the L1 of her students. She was aware that uptalk is common in colloquial English and was aware of the phenomenon at the time of the data collection, and Lola claimed that using the intonation pattern made it easier for students to understand her. Although she did not consciously intend to accommodate to the L1 of her students, she did comment retrospectively that it may have been a subconscious accommodation. All the aforementioned explanations for the prevalence of high-rising final intonation patterns in SDS are likely differentially responsible for the observed trends. Also, the findings highlight the strength of the nuclear position in portraying communicative and pragmatic information in the SDS style.

Notes

1 Lola ($t(191.28)=9.98$, $p<0.001$), Alejandra ($t(206.73)=5.51$, $p<0.001$), Tammy ($t(248)=2.65$, $p=0.009$)
2 The number of observations used in all independent sample t-tests was 250 ($n=250$), and the p-value to determine significance was set at <0.05 for all statistical tests.
3 An asterisk after a participant's name, a dependent variable, or a figure caption indicates statistical significance.
4 $t(234.25)=-1.85$, n.s.
5 The number of observations used for LMEMs in between-subject analyses on the effect of speech style was 1000 ($n=1000$).
6 $F(2.06)=-0.722$, n.s., 95% CI $[-1.7, 0.2656]$
7 Lola ($t(248)=-9.04$, $p<0.001$), Alejandra ($t(248)=-9.59$, $p<0.001$), Kate ($t(231.45)=-8.56$, $p<0.001$), Tammy ($t(233.92)=-6.61$, $p<0.001$)
8 $F(11.91)=3.076$, $p=<0.001$, 95% CI $[1.3, 4.82]$.
9 Lola ($t(248)=-12.35$, $p<0.001$), Alejandra ($t(248)=-12.28$, $p<0.001$), Kate ($t(248)=-10.19$, $p<0.001$), Tammy ($t(248)=-0.87$, $p<0.001$)
10 $F(11.71)=55.588$, $p<0.001$, 95% CI $[23.71, 87.46]$
11 $t(248.45)=-6.42$, $p<0.001$
12 $t(210.8)=-3.53$, $p<0.001$
13 $t(248)=-7.64$, $p<0.001$
14 $t(248)=-1.79$, n.s.
15 $F(4.39)=59.253$, $p=0.0364$, 95% CI $[3.76, 114.75]$
16 $t(248)=-2.78$, $p=0.006$
17 $t(248)=-6.14$, $p<0.001$
18 Alejandra ($t(248)=-0.24$, n.s.), Tammy ($t(248)=1.67$, n.s.)

19 $F(4.25)=0.337, p=0.04$, 95% CI [0.016, 0.658]
20 The number of observations used in chi-square tests of independence on the effect of speech style for each TA was 250 ($n=250$).
21 $\chi^2(5)=27.5, p<0.001$
22 $\chi^2(5)=33.5, p<0.001$
23 $\chi^2(5)=16.5, p<0.006$
24 $\chi^2(5)=6.2$, n.s.
25 $\chi^2(2, n=142)=7.528, p=0.023$
26 $\chi^2(2, n=136)=7.658, p=0.022$
27 $\chi^2(2, n=131)=8.9, p=0.012$
28 $\chi^2(2, n=84)=0.568$, n.s.
29 Lola (χ^2 (1, $n=142$)=6.945, $p=0.008$), Tammy (χ^2 (1, $n=131$)=5.564, $p=0.018$)
30 Alejandra (χ^2 (1, $n=136$)=2.4, n.s.), Kate: (χ^2 (1, $n=84$)=0.124, n.s.)
31 Lola (χ^2 (1, $n=142$)=1.785, n.s.), Alejandra (χ^2 (1, $n=136$)=0.063, n.s.), Kate (χ^2 (1, $n=84$)=0.565, n.s.), Tammy (χ^2 (1, $n=131$)=0.497, n.s.)
32 $F(7.34)=0.175, p=0.007$, 95% CI [0.048, 0.301]
33 $F(1.34)=-0.082$, n.s., 95% CI [−0.221, 0.057]
34 $\chi^2(4, n=97)=10.122, p=0.038$
35 Lola (χ^2 (4, $n=113$)=4.185 n.s.), Kate (χ^2 (4, $n=68$)=2.178, n.s.), Tammy (χ^2 (4, $n=92$)=6.452, n.s.)
36 $\chi^2(2, n=97)=6.897, p=0.032$
37 Lola (χ^2 (2, $n=113$)=4.088, n.s.), Kate (χ^2 (2, $n=68$)=0.609, n.s.), Tammy (χ^2 (2, $n=92$)=2.565, n.s.)
38 Lola (χ^2 (2, $n=113$)=2.458, n.s.), Alejandra (χ^2 (2, $n=97$)=3.44, n.s.), Kate (χ^2 (2, $n=68$)=0.747, n.s.), Tammy (χ^2 (2, $n=92$)=3.123, n.s.)
39 The number of observations used for LMEMs within SDS data alone was 600 ($n=600$).
40 $F(4.7)=-0.047, p=0.031$, 95% CI [−0.089, −0.004]
41 $F(2.85)=-0.099$, n.s., 95% CI [−0.215, 0.016]
42 $F(2.49)=0.035$, n.s., 95% CI [−0.009, 0.079]
43 $F(3.29)=0.108$, n.s., 95% CI [−0.009, 0.224]
44 In this context, experience refers to Alejandra's academic and professional preparation and background. Future discussions make reference to the TAs' familiarity with the course of instruction and student community. These concepts should not be conflated.

Reference

Gussenhoven, C. (2002a). Intonation and interpretation: Phonetics and phonology. In *Speech Prosody 2002, International Conference*. Retrieved from https://perso.limsi.fr/mareuil/control/gussenhoven.pdf

6 Individual differences and prosodic changes over time

Introduction

The results presented thus far reveal several prosodic features that characterize the SDS style. Overall, SDS prosody corresponds with features reported for formal, careful speech as well as accommodative and emphatic speech styles. As expected in presentational speech, the TAs spoke significantly slower when addressing students, with the exception of Kate. Articulation rate was not a significant variable distinguishing speech style, intensity was found to be statistically significant in both the within- and between-subject analyses, showing that the TAs spoke more loudly during SDS compared to conversational speech. With regard to pitch, F0 mean was significantly higher in SDS than in conversational speech for all four TAs, and F0 range was significantly wider in SDS for three of the four TAs. F0 mean and range were identified as statistically significant factors that differentiate SDS from conversational speech overall, indicating that F0 during SDS differs greatly from the pitch used during conversation. Phrases in SDS were relatively shorter than in conversation, evidenced by more pauses and BPM. Phrases in SDS most commonly contained one to three F0 peaks and consequently lacked the expected pre-nuclear rise patterns found in common declarative statements. However, two TAs produced significantly more F0 peaks per second in SDS when compared to conversational speech showing a lack of F0 suppression during SDS. From a more holistic perspective, these findings provide evidence of the variable prosodic productions in classroom speech, which are highly dependent on the environment in the classroom, the personality of the teacher, and the teacher's objectives and strategies. This chapter will explore in greater detail many of the variables that influence variation in prosodic behavior during SDS.

Prosodic variation across TAs

An investigation into how linguistic identity and professional training and experience relate to an individual's realization of prosody during SDS clarifies the quantitative findings presented in Chapter 5 and reveals new information about speech style and prosodic variation in natural speech environments. Findings from two different statistical queries on the data using within- and between-subject analyses are presented. The first looks at the effect of speech style within the NST (Lola and Alejandra) and NNST (Kate and Tammy) subgroups individually, and the second explores the effect of TL nativeness on the realization of prosodic features in the SDS data only. Results are compared with parallel analyses in the conversational speech style to verify their validity, and findings are interpreted according to information from background questionnaires and follow-up interviews.

Results

A series of LMEMs were used to explore the effect of speech style on prosody within NST and NNST subgroups.[1] Statistically significant differences were discovered between SDS and conversational speech for both NSTs and NNSTs with regard to intensity, pitch mean, pitch range, F0 peak frequency, and high-rising BPM.[2] Falling BPM was not significant for either group.[3] However, of more interest to the present exploration are the categories in which NSTs and NNSTs diverge, because a difference in the realization of a prosodic feature across speech styles for one group but not the other indicates a difference between groups.

Articulation rate was a statistically significant indicator of speech style in the NST subgroup according to a between-subject LMEM treating speech style as the independent factor,[4] but the feature was not significant for the NNST subgroup.[5] Figure 6.1 displays the average sylls/s uttered by NSTs and NNSTs in SDS and conversational speech. From the figure, it is clear that NSTs spoke considerably quicker during conversation than SDS, while the NNSTs used a more similar rate of speech in the two styles.

Looking just at the data collected from within the classroom, however, we find very few differences between the prosodic behaviors of NSTs and NNSTs. According to a series of LMEMs within SDS treating nativeness as an independent variable, most of the prosodic features were not significantly different between the NST and NNST subgroups. The nonsignificant factor groups included articulation rate, F0 mean, F0 range, F0 peak frequency, high-rising BPM, and falling BPM.[6] However, NSTs used a higher mean intensity in SDS on average when compared to

88 *Individual differences and changes over time*

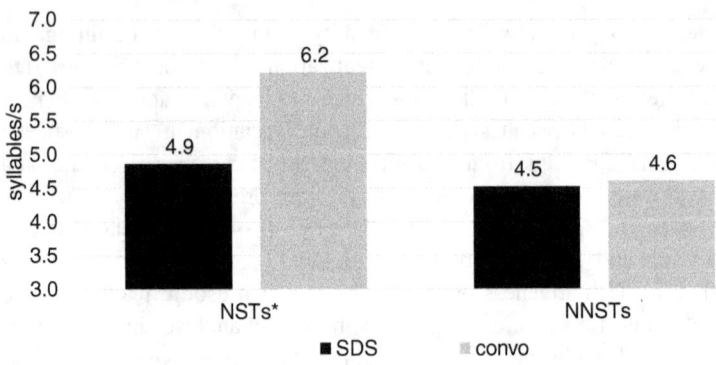

Figure 6.1 Articulation rate by nativeness in SDS and conversation.

NNSTs, as can be seen in Figure 6.2. The difference in average mean intensity between NSTs and NNSTs during SDS was found to be statistically significant through a LMEM.[7] The NSTs utilized a significantly louder voice in SDS by an average of almost 2 dB compared to their NNST peers.

To provide further evidence that the differences between NST and NNST subgroups are attributable to the SDS speech environment as opposed to other intervening variables, statistical models were employed to look for differences across subgroups in just the conversational speech

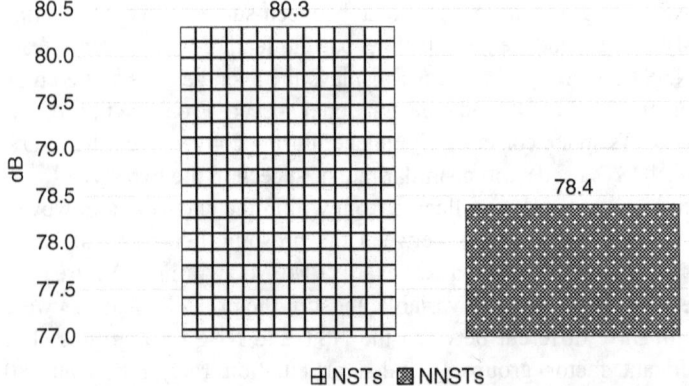

Figure 6.2 Mean intensity by nativeness in SDS and conversation.*

samples.[8] Six of the seven variables were not significantly different between groups according to LMEMs, including intensity, F0 mean, F0 range, F0 peak frequency, high-rising BPM, and falling BPM.[9] However, not surprisingly given the values displayed in Figure 6.1, NSTs used a significantly faster articulation rate in conversational speech compared to NNSTs, according to a LMEM.[10]

Discussion

These findings reveal that the change in articulation rate from conversational speech to SDS was far less extreme for NNSTs than NSTs. One explanation is the high speech rate ceiling of the NSTs compared to the NNSTs. Looking back at Figure 5.2, displaying individual average articulation rates in SDS and conversational speech, the NSTs spoke considerably faster in conversation than in SDS. Lola spoke an average of 1.7 sylls/s faster, and Alejandra spoke 1 sylls/s faster on average. Tammy's speech rate difference by speech style was also significant, but she only spoke 0.4 sylls/s faster in conversational speech. This shows that the meaningful difference in the data lies in the relative speed of conversational speech. Indeed, articulation rate in conversational speech was found to be statistically different between the NST and NNST subgroups, as presented above. This is the key in the analyses of individual subgroups as well. The NSTs spoke more swiftly in conversation than in SDS, but this difference was minimal for the NNSTs. This finding can, again, be attributed to the NSTs' higher speech rate ceiling in conversational speech and the consequently stark change to a slower pace in SDS. In fact, the groups did not differ greatly in speech rate during SDS as both used a rate of between 4.5 and 5 sylls/s overall when addressing students, and articulation rate was not a significant factor differentiating NSTs from NNSTs in the SDS data according to the analysis across subgroups. This shows that speech rate ceiling during conversation is the likely culprit for the significant finding across speech styles for NSTs.

The accelerated speech rate in the conversational speech of the NSTs may also be related to extralinguistic factors such as their use of the target language, time of day, the speakers' interest in the topic of conversation, etc. For instance, both pairs of research participants were friends prior to the data recording, but the NSTs used Spanish regularly in their social interactions and spoke particularly often with each other in Spanish. On the other hand, the NNSTs reported on the background questionnaire that they used Spanish less than 50% of the time with colleagues and friends, and their social interactions with each other were primarily in English. This explains the NSTs' accelerated articulation when speaking casually to each other and also the slower rate of NNST conversation. Once again, speech rate was relatively uniform during SDS, suggesting that conversational speech rate is not an accurate determiner of a teacher's rate of speech when addressing students in the L2 classroom. In conclusion, nativeness is not a factor determining rate of speech during SDS.

With regard to intensity, both NSTs and NNSTs used significantly higher mean intensity levels during SDS compared to conversation, although NSTs produced these manipulations to a greater degree. This shows that TAs spoke louder in the classroom than when addressing a colleague. However, in the SDS data alone, intensity was identified as a significant factor distinguishing NSTs from NNSTs. In other words, the TA's identity as a NS or NNS of the TL had a significant effect over the volume of their voice when addressing students. As a control, the same statistical model was run on the conversational speech data, and mean intensity was not statistically different between the groups. The fact that F0 intensity was significantly different for NSTs and NNSTs in SDS but not during conversational speech provides evidence for the assertion that intensity is produced differently by NSTs and NNSTs during SDS.

The significant finding for mean intensity in SDS across subgroups is consistent with the results from earlier analyses of individual TAs. As displayed in Figure 5.3, Lola and Alejandra both exhibited higher mean intensity in SDS compared to Kate and Tammy, and this was not the case in conversational speech. Because intensity is associated with clarity and oral comprehension, increased mean intensity in the NSTs' SDS can be explained by their desire to be understood by their students. In fact, in the follow-up interviews, both Lola and Alejandra stressed the importance of tailoring their speech so that students can understand them better. Lola admitted that her accent is difficult to understand, so she tries to speak more clearly to students. She said, "*Tampoco hablo natural porque quiero que me entiendan [los estudiantes]*" 'I also don't speak normally because I want them [the students] to understand me.' Alejandra also stressed the importance of comprehensibility.

The TAs' comments support the association between nativeness and increased intensity during SDS; however, other differences between the TAs may also be contributing to the significant findings for intensity. Referring back to the TAs' experience, at the time of data collection, both Lola and Alejandra were teaching the course for the first time and had been at the university for less than a year, while Kate and Tammy were veteran members of the department and had both taught the course several times previously. It is reasonable to believe that during their tenure at the university, Kate and Tammy developed awareness of the course and the proficiency level of the students and were, thus, accommodating to the students with regard to intensity in a different way when compared to Lola and Alejandra. In other words, it is possible that the NSTs' lack of familiarity with the course and level of the students caused their increased intensity output during SDS. This also relates back to the conversation in Chapter 3 about the prosodic adaptations that occur during FDS. Lola and Alejandra may have been treating their students as nonproficient users of the language, at least in the beginning of the semester, using increased intensity to accommodate to their listeners. In sum, although the significant findings suggest that NS or NNS identity plays a role in the production of average intensity during SDS, due to the likelihood that the outcome is influenced by the TAs' length of time in the department and experience teaching the course, nativeness cannot be confirmed as a factor in the realization of intensity during SDS.

Changes over the academic semester

While there are many features identified thus far that distinguish prosody in SDS from conversational speech, it is informative to explore how the TAs changed the type and extent of prosodic manipulations in their speech to students throughout the 15-week academic semester. Through both within- and between-subject analyses, it is confirmed that several prosodic variables changed significantly over time in SDS as the interlocutors gained familiarity with the students and the classroom dynamic matured. The results from statistical tests treating time in the semester as the independent variable are presented in this section, followed by a discussion considering findings from previous analyses and TA perspectives gathered through follow-up interviews.

Results

Treating time as the independent variable in within-subject analyses of SDS using chi-square tests and GLMs,[11] significant findings for the effect of time were discovered for at least one of the TAs in all of the prosodic variables tested with the exception of F0 peak frequency, where no significant trends were detected.[12]

Alejandra increased her average articulation rate over the three time points during the semester while the other three TAs, interestingly, decreased or maintained their average speech rate over time. Figure 6.3 shows the average speech rate utilized by each TA in SDS during each recording day. The dashed and dotted line represents Alejandra's speech, where a clear increase by day can be observed. According to results of GLMs, articulation rate across time in SDS was significant only for

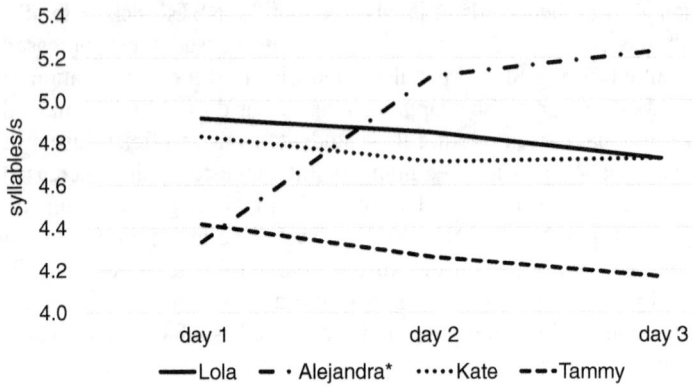

Figure 6.3 Articulation rate across time in SDS.

Alejandra.[13] The differences over time were not statistically significant for the other three TAs,[14] and the LMEM[15] for articulation rate by time in the semester across TAs was not significant.[16]

Additionally, both Lola and Alejandra decreased their mean intensity considerably from the first recording day to the second and more or less maintained that intensity during the third recording day. Kate also displayed a general decrease in mean intensity from day one to day three, while Tammy increased her mean intensity levels between the time points. Figure 6.4 displays the average mean intensity for each TA at different time points during SDS. Statistically significant differences for the effect of time in the semester were discovered for the variable of intensity in Lola and Alejandra's SDS,[17] but not for Kate or Tammy.[18] According to the LMEM across all participants, intensity was not a statistically significant factor for the effect of time in the semester.[19]

Regarding average F0 mean, pitch decreased across time for three of the four TAs during SDS, but more drastically in Alejandra's speech. Figure 6.5 presents the data for F0 mean across time for each TA in SDS. The dashed and dotted line represents Alejandra's speech, where a steep fall in F0 mean is observed from day one to day two. The change in F0 mean across time was only significant for Alejandra according to a series of GLMs.[20] The variable was not found to be significantly different across time in the between-subject analysis of the data of all participants combined.[21]

F0 range, on the other hand, became narrower across time in SDS for all four TAs. The average F0 range employed by each TA at the three time

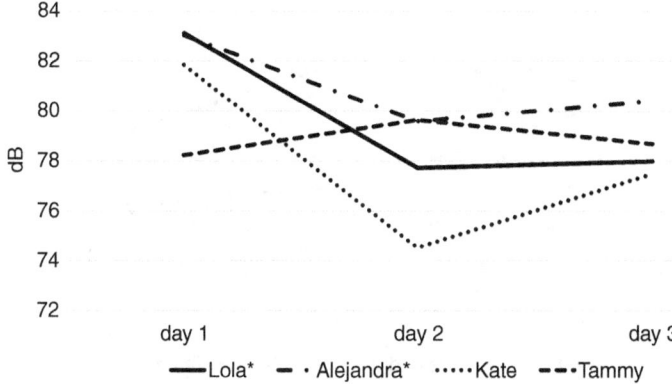

Figure 6.4 Mean intensity across time in SDS.

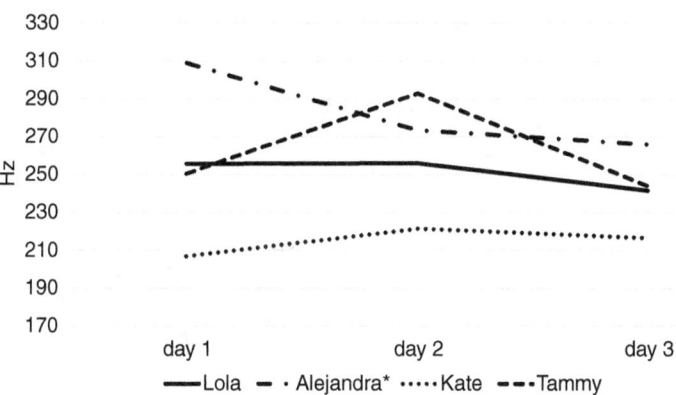

Figure 6.5 F0 mean across time in SDS.

points throughout the semester is displayed in Figure 6.6, and the overall average F0 range by recording day is shown in Figure 6.7. Differences in F0 range across time points were determined to be significant according to the within-subject analyses for Lola,[22] Alejandra,[23] and Tammy,[24] but not Kate.[25] In the between-subject analysis of time in the semester, F0 range was found to be statistically significant according to a LMEM.[26]

There were no observed patterns of pre-nuclear F0 rises over time in the SDS of Lola, Kate or Tammy, but Alejandra decreased her use of

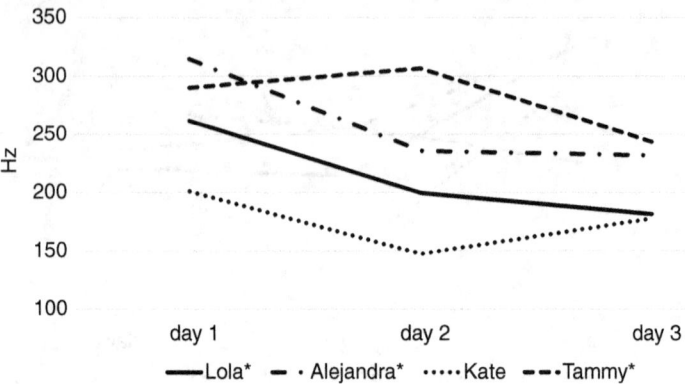

Figure 6.6 F0 range across time in SDS.

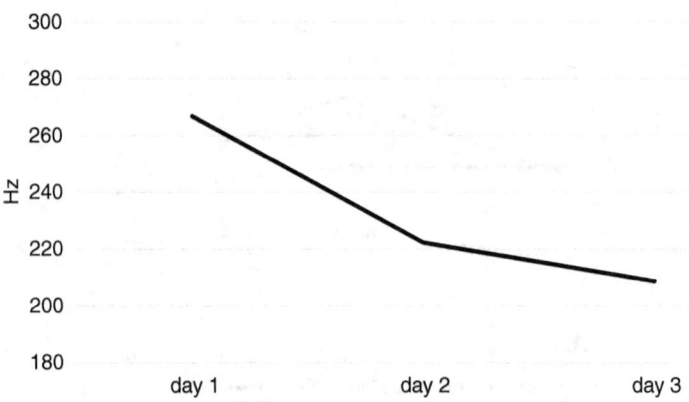

Figure 6.7 Overall F0 range across time in SDS.*

downstepped intonational contours and stress patterns associated with focused words from the first to third recording days. Indeed, a series of chi-square tests of independence revealed that time was a significant factor in the production of pre-nuclear F0 peak patterns for Alejandra,[27] but not the other three TAs.[28] The decreased frequency of pre-nuclear F0 rise patterns in Alejandra's SDS across time corresponded with an increase in intonational contours lacking rise patterns either due to the length of phrases or suppression of medial F0 migration. Alejandra's SDS phrases

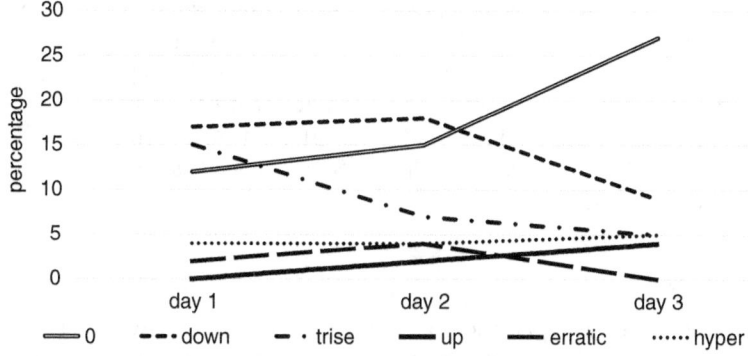

Figure 6.8 Alejandra's pre-nuclear F0 rise patterns across time in SDS.

categorized by pre-nuclear F0 rise pattern are presented in Figure 6.8 by recording day.

The findings for BPM across time were similarly inconclusive in the within-subject analyses, except for Lola. Changes in BPM frequency over time were significant for Lola,[29] but not for the other three TAs.[30] In her SDS, Lola used a considerable number of final high-rises in the beginning of the semester and reduced this frequency by the second recording day. She also reduced the number of final rises throughout the course of the semester. The frequency of final rises in Lola's SDS, on the other hand, increased over time. Figure 6.9 presents phrases categorized by BPM produced by Lola over the three time points in SDS. Downward

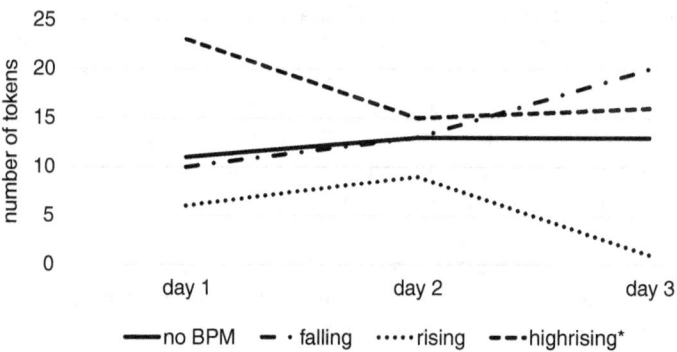

Figure 6.9 Lola's BPM across time in SDS.

trends in final rises (represented through the dotted and dashed lines) can be observed as well as an upward trend in final falling contours (represented through the dashed and dotted line). The downward trend in rising contours across time was seen only in Lola's data. The upward usage trend of falling contours is consistent with trends in Alejandra and Kate's SDS, but not Tammy's. LMEMs for the effect of time on the factors of high-rising BPM and falling BPM in SDS between-subjects were not significant.[31]

Discussion

At the onset of an academic semester, the relationship between teachers and students is not yet established, and the classroom dynamic is volatile. Over time, teachers become more aware of the students' proficiency level and comprehension skills, and the students get to know the teacher's personality and style. Because discourse information and pragmatic messages are conveyed through prosody, manipulations at the prosodic level are prone to flux as teachers and students become more familiar with one another and the course. This was indeed the case for the research participants with regard to F0 range, the only significant variable affected by time in the semester across all TAs. All four TAs used a wider F0 range during the third week of the semester (recording day one) compared to nearly two months later during week 10 (recording day three), as displayed in Figure 6.7.

Discourse cues and special emphasis are portrayed through pitch manipulation, as described previously. According to the follow-up interviews, all four TAs prioritize pedagogical objectives such as emphasizing key concepts and target words, and this is evidenced through the systematic realization of higher F0 mean and wider F0 range in SDS compared to conversation. Kate talked about the importance of "reinforcing grammar points" through "slowness and deliberate speech." Although Kate did not specifically refer to pitch, it is a recognized factor in the expression of special emphasis and focus. However, prosodic cues related to discourse marking and emphasis contexts are not likely to change based on familiarity between teachers and students. In fact, these functions may become more frequent as curricular material becomes more challenging. This is the case in the intermediate course taught by the TAs, where topics like the subjunctive mode are introduced and practiced in detail. Therefore, the tonal influence of discourse cues and the expression of emphasis does not explain the significant change in F0 range across time points in SDS overall.

A more fitting explanation for the overall significant finding is the association between H tones and positive affect, such as kindness and friendliness.

As mentioned previously, in the follow-up interviews, the TAs expressed great concern in making their students feel comfortable during class by portraying themselves as approachable, with the exception of Kate. Alejandra talked about how she uses higher tones when speaking with students to empathize with them, *"para ... que sepan que quiero hablar con ellos, que soy nice"* 'so that they know I want to speak with them, that I'm nice.' Lola and Tammy also reported having such intentions during SDS. Tammy mentioned that if students are struggling, she tries to empathize with them by acknowledging their feelings and encourage them to keep going. Kate, on the other hand, is generally not worried with making her students feel comfortable or being approachable in class, but she emphasized being serious and calm with her students by suppressing H tones. Sentiments of affect are particularly poignant at seedling stages of relationships when the social dynamic is still being established and become less prominent as familiarity grows; therefore, Alejandra, Lola, and Tammy's emphasis on empathy is the likely cause of the significant findings for pitch range across time. The TAs used a widened F0 range in the beginning of the semester for affective purposes, then reduced their F0 range throughout the semester as the social dynamic settled. This explanation also accounts for the nonsignificant finding for Kate in the within-subject analysis of F0 range as an effect of time in the semester, as Kate did not report the intention of engendering an environment of empathy and friendliness while teaching.

With regard to significant factor groups from within-subject analyses, there were significant effects of time for five of the seven prosodic variables in Alejandra's SDS. Time in the semester, also related to comfort and familiarity, greatly influenced Alejandra's realization of articulation rate, intensity, F0 mean, F0 range, and pre-nuclear F0 rise patterns. As Alejandra got to know her students, she began speaking more quickly during class causing phonetic reduction evidenced by the decrease in intensity, reduction in pitch mean, and narrowing of pitch range. Faster speech is associated with F0 suppression, which is seen in the decrease in frequency of expected pre-nuclear F0 rise patterns over time in Alejandra's SDS. In fact, the TA produced longer phrases containing more lexically-stressed words from day one to day three, showing that the absence of pre-nuclear F0 rise patterning is due to F0 suppression as opposed to an increase in shorter phrases over time. In the follow-up interviews, Alejandra explained that she accommodates to her interlocutors subconsciously, even though she reflects on her own behavior consciously. She admitted that she changes her speech when talking to students, foreigners, and even friends who use different dialects of Spanish, although she makes efforts to minimize these accommodations. As time passed in her class, Alejandra reduced the strength of her prosodic accommodations.

Lola also decreased volume and reduced F0 range over time in SDS, although there were not significant findings for the effect of time on Lola's articulation rate, F0 mean, or pre-nuclear F0 rise patterns. While Lola spoke more softly and used a more reduced pitch range as the semester progressed, she did not quicken the pace of her speech or reduce her intonation. Lola did, however, restrain the use of final rising and high-rising boundary movement and increase her use of falling boundary movement over time. As discussed earlier, Lola claimed that her high-rising tendency served the purpose of emphasizing an important item for the students or aiding in their comprehension. The decrease in high-rising BPM and narrowing in F0 range over time in Lola's SDS is evidence of an increase in familiarity between the TA and her students as she gained awareness of her students' comprehension abilities, and she was able to rely less on boundary pitch manipulations and L1 transfer for communication.

With regard to intensity, the significant changes over time in Alejandra and Lola's SDS confirm the earlier observation that the NSTs were accommodating their speech to the level of their interlocutors in the beginning of the semester. Without prior experience teaching intermediate Spanish, it is possible that Alejandra and Lola approached their classes with the idea that the students would have difficulty understanding their Spanish. Just like a fully proficient language user speaking to someone with limited proficiency, they intuitively spoke louder with their new students. Then, as they became more familiar with their students between the third week and seventh week of the semester, they adjusted their speech volume.

With the exception of F0 range in Tammy's SDS, none of the prosodic variables were significantly correlated with time in the semester for Kate and Tammy, compared to significant changes across time in a number of prosodic correlates in Lola and Alejandra's SDS. As per previous discussions pertaining to the influence of TL nativeness on SDS prosody, it is possible that TL nativeness played a role in the changes observed over time for NSTs. It may have taken the NSTs longer to gauge the level of language grading needed to effectively communicate with their students. NNSTs, on the other hand, empathize with the students' L2 learning processes as they were once students of Spanish themselves, so they may have more quickly judged the students' level. This explanation is supported by the comments of the TAs, as the NSTs were concerned that the students would not understand their particular Spanish accents, and this was not a concern of the NNSTs.

However, differences across subgroups can also be explained by the TAs' familiarity with the course of instruction and the particular community of students. The semester of recording was Lola and Alejandra's first time teaching the course while Kate and Tammy had taught the course several times prior. In fact, Kate was Head TA of the course that semester,

Individual differences and changes over time 99

speaking to her knowledge of and experience with the course material. Prior experience teaching a course has many advantages. In the follow-up interview, Kate explained that she typically has a better command of course material after teaching it once. Moreover, Lola said that an advantage of teaching a course for a second or subsequent time is that the teacher is aware of the level of the students. This observation by Lola was made two years following the semester of recording, after she had taught the course several more times. Familiarity with course material and the student community, therefore, is a logical explanation for the significant effects of time in the semester on prosodic correlates in the speech of Lola and Alejandra and the absence of significant effects in the speech of Kate and Tammy, with the exception of F0 range, which was comparable across all four TAs.

Notes

1 The number of observations used for LMEMs within individual subgroups was 500 ($n = 500$).
2 Intensity: NSTs ($F(159.34) = 2.97$, $p < 0.001$, 95% CI [2.508, 3.432]), NNSTs ($F(16.48) = 3.181$, $p < 0.001$, 95% CI [1.642, 4.72]); Pitch mean: NSTs ($F(332.05) = 63.235$, $p < 0.001$, 95% CI [56.417, 70.054]), NNSTs ($F(172.22) = 47.941$, $p < 0.001$, 95% CI [40.763, 55.119]); Pitch range: NSTs ($F(46.77) = 56.98$, $p < 0.001$, 95% CI [40.61, 73.35]), NNSTs ($F(48.02) = 61.527$, $p < 0.001$, 95% CI [44.082, 78.972]); F0 peak frequency: NSTs ($F(6.26) = 0.276$, $p = 0.013$, 95% CI [0.059, 0.493]), NNSTs ($F(12.35) = 0.398$, $p = 0.001$, 95% CI [0.175, 0.621]); High-rising BPM: NST ($F(9.17) = 0.2$, $p = 0.002$, 95% CI [0.07, 0.33]), NNSTs ($F(4.63) = 0.16$, $p = 0.033$, 95% CI [0.014, 0.308])
3 NSTs ($F(.55) = -0.051$, n.s., 95% CI [-0.188, 0.085]), NNSTs ($F(1.17) = -0.084$, n.s., 95% CI [-0.24, 0.069])
4 $F(119.98) = -2.359$, $p < 0.001$, 95% CI [-1.603, -1.115]
5 $F(.69) = -0.084$, n.s., 95% CI [-0.285, 0.116]
6 Articulation rate: $F(2.07) = -0.343$, n.s., 95% CI [-0.811, 0.125]; F0 mean: $F(0.98) = -28.278$, n.s., 95% CI [-84.329, 27.77]; F0 range: $F(0.03) = -9.76$, n.s., 95% CI [-122.17, 102.65]; F0 peak frequency: $F(0) = -0.001$, n.s., 95% CI [-0.414, 0.4]; High-rising BPM: $F(0.03) = -0.02$, n.s., 95% CI [-0.245, 0.203]; Falling BPM: $F(.3) = -0.06$, n.s., 95% CI [-0.276, 0.155]
7 $F(5.29) = 1.91$, $p = 0.022$, 95% CI [-3.54, -0.279]
8 The number of observations used for LMEMs within conversational speech data alone was 400 ($n = 400$).
9 Intensity: $F(1.53) = -2.119$, n.s., 95% CI [-5.491, 1.252]; F0 mean: $F(.6) = -12.984$, n.s., 95% CI [-45.933, 19.966]; F0 range: $F(0.15) = -14.308$, n.s., 95% CI [-86.233, 57.616]; F0 peak frequency: $F(0.14) = -0.129$, n.s., 95% CI [-0.799, 0.541]; High-rising BPM: $F(0.4) = 0.049$, n.s., 95% CI [-0.103, 0.2]; Falling BPM: $F(0.15) = -0.035$, n.s., 95% CI [-0.216, 0.146]
10 $F(24.32) = -1.618$, $p < 0.001$, 95% CI [-2.262, -0.973]
11 The number of observations used for chi-square tests of independence and least squares general linear models on time in the semester for each TA was 150 ($n = 150$).

Individual differences and changes over time

12 Lola ($F(0.07)=-0.038$, n.s.), Alejandra ($F(0.79)=0.09$, n.s.), Kate ($F(0.61)=0.108$, n.s.), Tammy ($F(0.67)=0.093$, n.s.)
13 $F(11.28)=0.45, p<0.001$
14 Lola ($F(0.62)=-0.096$, n.s.), Kate ($F(0.23)=-0.052$, n.s.), Tammy ($F(1.34)=-0.125$, n.s.)
15 The number of observations used for LMEMs on the effect of time in the semester across all TAs was 600 ($n=600$).
16 $F(0.11)=0.044$, n.s., 95% CI [−0.389, 0.478]
17 Lola ($F(97.93)=-22.571, p<0.00$), Alejandra ($F(53.88)=-1.302, p<0.001$)
18 Kate ($F(0.28)=-0.683$, n.s.), Tammy ($F(0.47)=0.227$, n.s.)
19 $F(5.51)=-1.457$, n.s., 95% CI [−3.43, 0.519]
20 Lola ($F(3.38)=-7$, n.s.), Alejandra ($F(26.72)=-21.435$, $p<0.001$), Kate ($F(3.52)=4.89$, n.s.), Tammy ($F(0.31)=-3.23$, n.s.)
21 $F(1.48)=-6.694$, n.s., 95% CI [−24.211, 10.824]
22 $F(21.07)=-40.014, p<0.001$
23 $F(20.07)=-41.37, p<0.001$
24 $F(4.23)=-23.346, p=0.042$
25 $F(1.61)=0.207$, n.s
26 $F(4.39)=59.253, p=0.036$, 95% CI [−51.756, −6.407]
27 $\chi^2(10)=24.694, p=0.006$
28 Lola ($\chi^2(10)=11.387$, n.s.), Kate ($\chi^2(10)=6.926$, n.s.), Tammy ($\chi^2(10)=11.489$, n.s.)
29 $\chi^2(4, n=113)=11.91, p=0.018$
30 Alejandra ($\chi^2(4, n=97)=4.162$, n.s.), Kate ($\chi^2(4, n=68)=8.459$, n.s.), Tammy ($\chi^2(4, n=92)=6.545$, n.s.)
31 High-rising BPM: $F(.04)=-0.02$, n.s., 95% CI [−0.12, 0.08]; Falling BPM: $F(1.34)=-0.082$, n.s., 95% CI [−0.221, 0.057]

7 Conclusions, implications, and future research

Introduction

Gathering evidence from the quantitative and qualitative analyses presented in Chapters 5 and 6, it is possible to paint a comprehensive picture of SDS as it differs from conversational speech. While there are patterns that are consistent in the SDS style across TAs, there are some prosodic variables that are more and less susceptible to variation, and this variation is differential given the individual TAs and time in the semester. Overall, these findings confirm earlier descriptions of didactic speech (Faraco, Kida, Barbier, & Piolat, 2002; Gerard & Dahan, 1995; Rao, 2011); however, there are several novel discoveries that add to our knowledge of the speech style.

Conclusions

The TAs spoke louder and used a higher pitch register and wider pitch range in SDS. Increased intensity is attributed to the presentational speech style and accommodative strategies. It is common for individuals addressing a group of people to use louder speech. Similarly, people with advanced language proficiency tend to speak louder when addressing those with less advanced proficiency. Exaggerated F0 mean and range discovered in the SDS data are explained by attention-getting strategies and the portrayal of affect, which goes in line with Gussenhoven's (2002) and Hirschberg's (2002) accounts of the biological codes that are universally responsible for pitch variation. Phrases in SDS were shorter and riddled with pauses, resulting in fewer expected pre-nuclear F0 rise patterns. The ubiquity of short, choppy phrases in SDS confirms hypotheses based on Willis's (1992) description of the speech style and the observation, made by Tobin, King, Henderson, Bellocchi, and Ritchie (2016), that physiological effects of teaching cause irregular prosodic patterns and frequent pauses. Utterance-medial F0 suppression was less common in SDS compared to conversational speech, and Lola and Kate exhibited drastic increases in the number of F0 peaks they produced per second during SDS compared to conversational speech, a finding which is attributed to their self-reported introverted personalities. In order to hold the students' attention and engage them, Lola and Kate used more exaggerated pitch modulations as a parent would when speaking to a baby.

With regard to pre-nuclear F0 rise patterns, downstepping was the most common shape of pre-nuclear rises in SDS, although it was less frequent during the speech style when compared to conversational speech. This can be attributed to the naturalistic speech elicited in the present investigation. In spontaneous speech occurring within the L2 classroom, an increase in shorter phrases and more frequent pauses limit opportunities for expected pre-nuclear rise patterns to occur. However, while the incidence of downstepping was reduced in the SDS data compared to conversational speech, phrases during SDS seemed to be downstepped relative to one another. An *ip* would often be scaled to a lower pitch than the preceding *ip* within a larger IP, indicating the continuation of an idea. Therefore, although downstepping was not identified as a clear feature of SDS based on the present analyses, it is possible that it is occurring on a more discursive level during SDS.

The consistent features of SDS that were identified in this investigation are similar to those of FDS and IDS according to descriptions by Biersack, Kempe, and Knapton (2005) and Bergeson, Miller, and McCune (2006), involving phrase segmentation, intensity, F0 mean, and F0 range. This comparison confirms many of the explanations posited in Chapter 3 for the prosodic modifications occurring in L2 classrooms. For instance, the expression of discourse cues and pragmatic messages are pervasive in IDS as well as SDS, so it is logical to associate prosodic correlates that are common across the two speech styles with such communicative functions. What's more, exaggerated articulation in the SDS data, evidenced through increased intensity, slower speech rate (for three TAs), higher F0 mean, and wider F0 range, among others, can be associated with intelligibility and comprehension as in Kuhl et al.'s (1997) study on phonetic features of IDS. These features contribute to what can be conceived as clear speech, while also providing students cues as far as word parsing and relative importance of constituents in an utterance.

However, while reduced speech rate is often identified as a characteristic of FDS and IDS (Scarborough, Brenier, Zhao, Hall-Lew, & Dmitrieva, 2007) as well as didactic speech styles (Faraco et al., 2002; Gerard & Dahan, 1995), speech rate was not consistently slower in SDS than in the conversational speech data presented here. Three TAs used a

Conclusions, implications, and future research 103

significantly slower articulation rate during SDS than conversational speech, while Kate used a more accelerated rate of speech in SDS. However, it is possible that Kate's rapid speech rate has other explanations. First of all, Kate described the class she was teaching that semester as "stressful." According to Tobin et al.'s study, stressful emotions while teaching can have physiological effects on speech prosody, particularly pacing. It is possible that Kate's speech rate SDS is explained by the heightened emotions that she reported feeling that semester. Therefore, given the statistically significant findings for speech rate as an effect of speech style for the other TAs, it can be concluded that articulation is generally slower in SDS, but it cannot be considered a systematic feature of the speech style.

Additionally, a novel finding is the prominence of boundary marking during SDS, as both falling and high-rising BPM were utilized more frequently by the TAs in SDS compared to conversational speech. The TAs utilized more final high-rises during talk turns involving instruction or administrative functions to signal non-finality or engage the students by posing rhetorical (declarative) questions. Both the correlation between BPM and utterance purpose as well as between falling BPM and utterance purpose were significant for Alejandra. She held a Master's degree in L2 Spanish Education at the time of data collection, while the other three TAs had not formally studied education, distinguishing Alejandra from the others with regard to teaching expertise. It is possible that Alejandra's use of particular BPM styles during different instructional episodes to communicate discourse cues and pragmatic meaning is evidence of her L2 teacher education and experience.

In addition, throughout the data of all TAs, high-rising BPM correlated with instructional and administrative utterances. This finding may be attributed to didactic functions, as evidenced through the TAs' comments describing the use of high-rises as an effort to communicate discourse cues to the students, e.g., that it is their turn to respond, to emphasize an important word or phrase, or to engage the students by posing rhetorical questions; a linguistic phenomenon explained by Hirschberg (2002) as a violation of biological codes that communicates a unique message. However, the use of high-rising BPM during instruction and administration may also be influenced by the NSTs' linguistic accommodation to the students' L1, as uptalk has been reported extensively as a feature of English dialects (Bradford, 1997; Cruttenden, 2007; Guy & Vonwiller, 1989; Inoue, 2006; Podesva, 2011; Ritchart & Arvaniti, 2014; Warren, 2005, 2016). This interpretation is substantiated by comments from Lola, who claimed in the follow-up interviews that she utilized prosodic features of English, such as high-rising phrase boundaries, to accommodate to the

L1 of the students. This falls in line with Bradford's (1997) assertion that high-rising BPM can be used by speakers to promote feelings of camaraderie.

With regard to TL nativeness, speech rate was significantly slower in SDS compared to conversational speech for NSTs, though this finding is explained by the speakers' rapid speech rate during conversational speech and the relatively slower conversational speech rate of the NNSTs. In fact, the two groups actually used similar rates of articulation during SDS. Similarly, intensity differences were more extreme for the NST subgroup, and one possible explanation for this finding is the NSTs' fear that the students would not understand their speech. However, the NSTs may also have drastically graded their speech more than the NNSTs due to the NSTs' lack of familiarity with the course, the level of the students, and the campus community. This hypothesis is supported by the findings from analyses for the effect of time in the semester on prosodic correlates of SDS.

NSTs reduced their accommodation strategies over the three time points to a greater extent than the NNSTs, with the exception of changes in F0 range that were common across all TAs. TL nativeness is one possible explanation for the prosodic changes across time for NSTs compared to NNSTs. The NSTs themselves explained that they use acoustic accommodations in SDS due to their concern that the students would have difficulty understanding their native accents. Nevertheless, changes across time in Lola and Alejandra's SDS are more likely attributable to the individuals' lack of experience in the department at that time. As Lola and Alejandra became more familiar with the students and the course throughout the semester, they adjusted their prosodic adaptations to their audience. The change across time for the two TAs, to the exclusion of Kate and Tammy who had both spent a number of years in the department and taught the course several times previously, highlights the influence of familiarity with the course and students on the type and degree of prosodic modifications in SDS.

Despite the influences of the social community of the L2 classroom, individual variation, and TL nativeness, the trends in SDS are similar across speakers on the whole, and especially later in the semester when other intervening variables have minimized effects. The prosodic behaviors of NSTs in SDS converged with those of their NNSTs colleagues over time, showing that there are prosodic correlates of SDS that are common across TAs, particularly after accounting for the influence of time in the semester. There was a significant decrease in F0 range throughout the semester across the data overall, showing consistency across speakers. The fact that the TAs changed in similar ways over the semester regarding pitch modulation but not in other features like articulation rate exposes systematicity in SDS. These findings provide evidence for the assertion that SDS is its own unique speech style. The particular prosodic modifications used during SDS are attributed to personality, attitude, and emotion, as well as general articulatory strategies used to aid oral comprehension, attract students' attention, and communicate discourse cues. In conclusion, these findings support the classification of SDS as a unique speech style and offer assurance to students that different types of teachers, NSs and NNSs alike, actually behave quite similarly in class with regard to speech prosody.

Implications of the findings

Pedagogy

Up until now, our knowledge of the prosodic features of didactic speech had derived largely from impressionistic accounts and laboratory-based studies. The present analysis of the naturally-occurring in-class speech data of four different TAs verified the prosodic correlates of SDS observed in previous research, while also revealing nuanced variations across individuals and according to time in the semester. This newfound information guides future research on didactic speech styles as well as the effectiveness of oral instructed input. If we can isolate the prosodic accommodations that improve the effectiveness of classroom instruction (e.g., by facilitating TL comprehension or improving the social dynamic), we can use that information to train future L2 educators. Additionally, because input is so crucial to the L2 learning process, it is valuable to explore the potentially impeding effects of prosodic accommodations. The novel findings from the present investigation set the stage for future research of this nature.

Additionally, the evidence presented in this book pinpoint prosodic characteristics of L2 input, and it will now be valuable to explore how the students feel, respond, and perhaps benefit from the particular modifications used in teacher talk. For instance, it is imaginable that students would appreciate the modifications because they aid in comprehension, or on the contrary, that students would resent the modifications because they do not represent real world natural speech. Therefore, by establishing consistent features of SDS prosody and identifying those features that are more susceptible to variation, this investigation provides a more empirical basis for the creation of oral stimuli that resemble naturally-occurring classroom speech. Such stimuli could be utilized in follow-up studies on student perception of prosodic modifications of SDS.

What's more, evidence presented in this book sheds light on the influence of teacher training on prosodic behavior during SDS. Alejandra utilized more prosodic cues during teacher talk overall, and she consistently used falling and high-rising BPM to communicate messages unique to the objectives of the speech act. Both Alejandra's use of pitch manipulation in certain pedagogical contexts and her meta-awareness of her behavior can be linked to her prior teaching experiences and teacher preparation, as this is the one variable that distinguishes Alejandra from the other three TAs. This provides further evidence for the assertion that prosodic modifications can be taught, as Biersack et al. (2005) resolved in their study comparing prosodic accommodations in IDS and FDS. Additionally, meta-awareness of SDS prosody is shown to allow teachers to make changes to their teaching practice (Tobin et al., 2016). Therefore, training programs that raise TA awareness of their use of prosody while teaching may be particularly valuable.

On a similar note, trends in the data also reveal the influence of familiarity with the course and university community on language grading. Because Lola and Alejandra were relatively new to the university, their prosodic accommodations were more extreme at the beginning of the semester but stabilized by the tenth week. These changes were not observed for the other two TAs who had taught the course previously, with the exception of F0 range. This finding suggests the importance of TA training and preparation, specifically familiarizing new teachers to the learner community. There are several ways to expose new teachers to the course and university community prior to their first day of teaching, such as incorporating classroom observations of seasoned TAs and mock teaching activities with real students as components of new teacher orientation programs.

It is evident from the analyses presented here that while several factors contribute to the production of prosody during SDS, nativeness is less likely to be a key motivator for variation across speakers. In most cases, NSTs and NNSTs converged over time in SDS with regard to prosody, and divergences are explained by other differences between individuals. What's more, despite considerable variation in articulation rate between the two groups in the conversational speech setting, they used comparable rates of speech in the classroom. This observation supports the assertion that ceiling articulation rate in conversation is not a relevant factor distinguishing NNSTs from NSTs in SDS. This is useful information for L2 students pursuing classes with different types of speakers.

Finally, evidence shows that SDS is not representative of conversational speech in the TL, which may explain why some students feel uncomfortable or incompetent using the TL outside of the classroom. Because teacher talk represents one particular style of prosody, it is advisable for teachers to be aware of the prosodic qualities that the students are exposed to in their classes and to administer course activities that involve authentic speech produced in different social contexts and speech registers. In order to do this, L2 curricula should include TL practice through movies and music, YouTube videos, field trips or excursions, interviews with scholars or practitioners using video chat technology, and programs matching students with local or international conversation partners.

Methodology

Findings from the current investigation also have implications for research involving mixed methods and naturalistic data elicitation. The use of mixed methods including both quantitative and qualitative measures proved to be very revelatory. While the exploration of prosodic trends through frequencies and measures of central tendency were useful, statistical testing uncovered the relative strength of associations between independent variables and prosodic correlates. Comparing findings from quantitative analyses with qualitative data served to both verify and debunk explanations for the observed trends and, in many cases, revealed the detailed underpinnings of variation across TAs in SDS. The follow-up interviews were particularly informative in identifying the underlying causes of prosodic behaviors. These observations provide support for Llurda's (2014) recommendation that researchers should consider multiple perspectives in the analysis of natural, spontaneous speech styles. Specifically given the complex social dynamic of the L2 classroom, these findings expose the value of consulting qualitative evidence when interpreting quantitative data deriving from naturally-occurring speech.

Results from this investigation also highlight the importance of naturalistic speech elicitation methodologies in representing naturally-occurring speech styles. Detailed findings such as increased phrasal segmentation, varied articulation rate, and the frequency of high-rising BPM were only exposed because of the data collection methodology employed here. Because similar behaviors related to these prosodic correlates were not identified in previous studies on didactic speech utilizing laboratory-based data (Rao, 2011), it can be concluded that they were spurred by the natural, spontaneous speech style and the interactional environment of L2 classrooms. Indeed, many of the prosodic behaviors observed during SDS were influenced by the presence of students. This confirms evidence from studies on IDS and FDS that found differences in speech behavior depending on the presence of real or imagined interlocutors (Uther, Knoll, & Burnham, 2007). Therefore, in order to capture prosody of SDS and other natural-occurring speech styles, it is necessary to observe speakers in their natural speech environment, in this case, within the walls of the L2 classroom.

Future research directions

Though this research uncovered valuable information about SDS prosody, there is much more to discover regarding individual variation. There was considerable individual variation between the TAs participating in this investigation, although the effects of these variables were accounted for wherever possible through qualitative evidence. The individual differences did not affect within-subject analyses but limited the types of between-subject analyses that could be used. In future research, it would be useful to run a pilot study to increase comparability between participants in order to increase the power of statistical tests and reveal more conclusive results. It should be noted, however, that when working with human subjects in authentic speech environments, variability is inevitable. An alternative remedy would be to expand the sample population in order to increase generalizability of trends.

Additionally, the NST and NNST subgroups differed with respect to TL nativeness as well as experience teaching the course and familiarity with the students. For this reason, it was unclear in the quantitative data whether prosodic differences between the two groups were due to TL nativeness or other confounding variables. In future studies, it would be useful to control for linguistic and extralinguistic factors other than TL nativeness in speaker groups in order to be able to make more confident conclusions as to the effect of TL nativeness on SDS prosody. This could be done through a more comprehensive screening process and a greater number of subjects involved in the analyses. Furthermore, it would be valuable to include FL Spanish teachers with other linguistic backgrounds such as heritage language (HL) users. With growing interest in the field about HL use, particularly regarding pronunciation, it is time to explore how these speakers resemble or differ from other types of speakers in the context of classroom teaching.

The consideration of visual data would also enhance the scope of the present investigation. While the audio speech samples provided a wealth of information as to the TAs' actual phonetic behavior, gestural movements and facial expressions may expose further clues about the intention of speakers and context of interactions. McNeill, Levy, and Duncan (2015) identify gesture and prosody as two central components of discourse organization and recommend that they be analyzed in tandem to depict discourse. For this reason, a suggested follow-up study to the research presented in this book is one that employs principles of CA in the exploration of prosody by annotating speech transcripts using video recordings in order to include fine-grained details about interactions. A study of this nature would undoubtedly reveal further information about pragmatic meaning of intonation during SDS and aspects of the interactive L2 classroom space that influence speech prosody.

In future analyses of this nature, it may be illuminating to experiment with applying the AM theory, particularly in the analysis of BPM. As described in Chapter 2, because of the highly variable and gradient nature of the speech data used for analysis here, it was determined that the AM framework was not the right fit for the objectives and scope of the present investigation. That being said, there is value in bridging the gap between theoretical models of phonology and acoustic analyses of phonetic data rooted in social interaction, as recent research has pointed out (Hall, 2015). A more in-depth study utilizing the notation conventions of SP_ToBI would reveal further nuances about pre-tonic tones, downstepping and upstepping, and BPM, such as final lengthening and peak alignment. This type of analysis would extend the contributions of the present project.

The present investigation also opens the door for reception studies that gauge the effectiveness of prosodic modifications. Now that we have a clearer picture of SDS prosody, it is valuable to explore how students respond to the accommodations utilized in the L2 classroom. For instance, one could imagine a study using online processing technology such as event related potentials to show how sensitive students are to specific types of prosodic cues and modifications. Alternatively, the evidence presented in this book informs a future study that uses judgment tests with categories of adjectives describing how sentences produced with particular prosodic qualities make listeners feel. The experimental stimuli could be acoustically manipulated in Praat software to develop duplets of utterances, one exhibiting prosodic features of SDS and the other exhibiting conversational prosody. In this way, results of the study would point to the effect of prosodic cues in isolation, controlling for the effects of gender, native-speaker status, syntactic structure, and other potentially confounding variables. Such experiments involving student perception of prosodic modifications that occur during SDS would shed light on the consequences of accommodations and, thus, the relevance of SDS prosody as a topic in L2 teacher training programs.

References

Bergeson, T. R., Miller, R. J., & McCune, K. (2006). Mothers' speech to hearing-impaired infants and children with cochlear implants. *Infancy, 10*(3), 221–240. doi: 10.1207/s15327078in1003_2

Biersack, S., Kempe, V., & Knapton, L. (2005). Fine-tuning speech registers: a comparison of the prosodic features of child-directed and foreigner-directed speech. *Interspeech*, 2401–2404. doi: 10.13140/2.1.2133.5049

Bradford, B. (1997). Upspeak in British English. *English Today, 13*(3), 29–36. doi: 10.1017/S0266078400009810

Cruttenden, A. (2007). Intonational diglossia: A case study of Glasgow. *Journal of the International Phonetic Association, 37*(2), 257–274. doi: 10.1017/S0025100307002915

Faraco, M., Kida, T., Barbier, M. L., & Piolat, A. (2002). Didactic prosody and notetaking in L1 and L2. In *Speech Prosody 2002, International Conference*.

Gerard, C., & Dahan, D. (1995). Durational variations in speech and didactic accent during reading. *Speech Communication, 16*(3), 293–311. doi: 10.1016/0167-6393(94)00060-N

Gussenhoven, C. (2002a). Intonation and interpretation: Phonetics and phonology. In *Speech Prosody 2002, International Conference*. Retrieved from https://perso.limsi.fr/mareuil/control/gussenhoven.pdf

Guy, G., & Vonwiller, J. (1989). The high rising tone in Australian English. In P. Collins, & D. Blair (Eds.), *Australian English: The language of a new society* (pp. 21–34). Queensland: University of Queensland Press.

Hall, K. C. (2015). Categorical segments, probabilistic models. In E. Raimy, & C. E. Cairns (Eds.), *The segment in phonetics and phonology* (pp. 129–148). Hoboken, NJ: Wiley-Blackwell. doi: 10.1002/9781118555491.ch6

Hirschberg, J. (2002). The pragmatics of intonational meaning. In *Speech Prosody 2002, International Conference*.

Inoue, F. (2006). Sociolinguistic characteristics of intonation. In Y. Kawaguchi, I. Fonágy, & T. Moriguchi (Eds.), *Prosody and syntax: Cross-linguistic perspectives* (pp. 197–223). Philadelphia, PA: John Benjamins. doi: 10.1075/ubli.3.12ino

Kuhl, P. K., Andruski, J. E., Chistovich, I. A., Chistovich, L. A., Kozhevnikova, E. V., Ryskina, V. L., Stolyarova, E. I., Sundberg, U., & Lacerda, F. (1997). Cross-language analysis of phonetic units in language addressed to infants. *American Association for the Advancemente of Science, 277*(5326), 684–686. doi: 10.1126/science.277.5326.684

Llurda, E. (2014). Non-native teachers and advocacy. In M. Bigelow, & J. Ennser-Kananen (Eds.), *The Routledge handbook of educational linguistics*, 105–116. doi: 10.4324/9781315797748

McNeill, D., Levy, E. T., & Duncan, S. D. (2015). Gesture in discourse. In D. Tannen, H. Hamilton, & D. Schiffrin (Eds.), *The handbook of discourse analysis* (2 ed., pp. 262–290). Hoboken, NJ: Wiley-Blackwell. doi: 10.1002/9781118584194.ch12

Podesva, R. J. (2011). Salience and the social meaning of declarative contours: Three case studies of gay professionals. *Journal of English Linguistics, 39*(3), 233–264. doi: 10.1177/0075424211405161

Rao, R. (2011). Intonation in spanish classroom-style didactic speech. *Journal of Teaching and Research, 3*, 31–75. doi: 10.4304/jltr.2.3.493-507

Ritchart, A., & Arvaniti, A. (2014). The form and use of uptalk in Southern Californian English. *Proceedings of Meetings on Acoustics, 20*.

Scarborough, R., Brenier, J., Zhao, Y., Hall-Lew, L., & Dmitrieva, O. (2007). An Acoustic Study of Real and Imagined Foreigner-Directed Speech. In J. Trouvain, & W. J. Barry (Eds.), *Proceedings of the 16th International Conference of* the *Phonetic Sciences* (pp. 2165–2168). Saarbruecken, Germany. doi: 10.1121/1.4781735

Tobin, K., King, D., Henderson, S., Bellocchi, A., & Ritchie, S. M. (2016). Expression of emotions and physiological change during teaching. *Cultural Studies of Science Education, 11*, 669–692. doi: 10.1007/s11422-016-9778-9

Uther, M., Knoll, M. A., & Burnham, D. (2007). Do you speak E-NG-L-I-SH? A comparison of foreigner- and infant- directed speech. *Speech Communication,* 2–7. doi: 10.1016/j.specom.2006.10.003

Warren, P. (2005). Patterns of late rising in New Zealand English: Intonational variation or intonational change? *Language Variation and Change, 17*, 209–230. doi: 10.1017/S095439450505009X

Warren, P. (2016). *Uptalk: The phenomenon of rising intonation.* Cambridge: Cambridge University Press. doi: 10.1017/CBO9781316403570

Willis, J. (1992). Inner and outer: Spoken discourse in the language classroom. In M. Coulthard (Ed.), *Advances in spoken discourse analysis* (pp. 162–182). London: Routledge. doi: 10.4324/9780203200063

Index

Page numbers in **bold** denote tables, those in *italics* denote figures.

absolute interrogatives 12, 18, 20
accommodation *see* speech accommodation
acoustic correlates, of stress and focus 13–17
acoustic prominence 9, 14, 70
adult-directed speech (ADS) 40, 41
Afro-Bolivian Spanish (ABS) 12
Andreeva, B. 30
Applied Linguistics 3
articulation rate: analysis of 60; calculating 13; comparisons between SDS and conversation 66–8, *67*, *68*, *79*, *80*; discussion 69–70; function of variations in 13–14; individual variation 87, *88*, 89–90; over time 91, *92*; as prosodic correlates of SDS 66–70; reduction in 4–5, 13, 35, 36, 69–70, 102
Árva, V. 38
Audience Design, Bell's model 39–40
Autosegmental-Metrical (AM) model 10–11, 109

baby babble *see* motherese
Barry, W. 30
Bell, A. 39
Bellocchi, A. 101
Bergeson, T.R. 40, 102
Biersack, S. 41–2, 102
boundary marking 21–2, 103; ways of 57
boundary pitch movement (BPM): analysis of 60; comparisons between SDS and conversation 79–82; correlation between BPM and utterance purpose 103; discussion 82–4; frequency in SDS and conversation *79*; individual variation 87, 89; over time 95–6; patterns coded in the data 58; pitch contour in SDS and conversation *79*; research recommendations 109; shapes in SDS and conversation *80*; utterance purpose in SDS *81*
Boves, L. 13
Bradford, B. 22, 104
Brazil, D. 34
broad focus declaratives 11–12, 16–17, 19–20, 58, 78
Brutt-Griffler, J. 38

Callahan, L. 38
Canagarajah, S. 37
Castilian Spanish *see* Peninsular Spanish
Charness, G. 60
child-directed speech (CDS) 18, 41, 42
Chomsky, N. 12
Christie, F. 34–5
classroom behaviours of L2 teachers 1–2, 8
cochlear implants 40
Communication Accommodation Theory (CAT) 39
contrastive focus 11–12, 15–17
conversation: comparisons with SDS

30, *67*, *68*, *71*, *72*, 75, *76*, 79, *80*, 86, *88*; F0 suppression in *31*, 74
Conversation Analysis (CA) 36, 108
correlates of stress and focus 13–17
Cots, J.M. 38
Coupland, N. 39
Crago, M. 34
Cruttenden, A. 33
Cuban Spanish 20
Cucchiarini, C. 13

Dahan, D. 36
deaccenting *see* F0 suppression
declarative intonation: broad focus *20*; contour patterns 31; variation in 19–21
de la Mota, C. 10, 17
Díaz, J.P. 38
didactic accent, definition 36
Discourse Analysis 35
discourse organization, gesture and prosody as central components of 108
downstepping 16, 19, 36, 58, 71, 76–8, 94, 102, 109
Duncan, S.D. 108
duration: as acoustic correlate of stress and focus 13–15; effect of context on 36; meaning of 8; phrasal segmentation criteria 57–8, 67, 75; *see also* articulation rate

emotional load, impact on phonetic strength 32–3
Eriks-Brophy, A. 34
Estebas Vilaplana, E. 10

fundamental frequency (F0): meaning of 8; *see also* F0 mean; F0 movement; F0 peak frequency; F0 pre-nuclear rise pattern; F0 range; F0 suppression
F0 mean: analysis of 60; comparisons between SDS and conversation 70–1, *72*; discussion 73–4; individual variation 86–7, 89; over time 92, *93*, 96–8
F0 movement: instructional phrases and 83; as phrase boundary cue 57; role in distinguishing declarative from interrogative utterances 19; types of words accompanied by 9
F0 peak frequency: discussion 77–8; comparisons between SDS and conversation 74–6, *75*, *76*; individual differences 87, 89; measurement of 60; over time 91
F0 pre-nuclear rise pattern: analysis of 60; discussion 78; comparisons between SDS and conversation 76–7; patterns coded in the data 58; over time 94, 97
F0 range: as acoustic correlate of stress and focus 15–17; analysis of 60; comparisons between SDS and conversation 70–2, *72*; discussion 73–4; individual variation 86–7, 89; over time 92–3, *94*, 96–9; F0 suppression: comparison of SDS with conversational speech 86, 102; contrastive focus and 16; in conversation *31*, 74; faster speech and 97; frequencies in different speech communities 12; introverted personality and 78, 102; Rao's discovery 11–12, 36; reduction and 31; in Spanish 16; in spontaneous speech 14, 31–2
Face, T.L. 10, 12, 14, 17, 20, 31–2, 36
Faraco, M. 36
Ferguson, C.A. 40
Fernald, A. 41
foreigner-directed speech (FDS) 40–2, 49, 69–70, 91, 102, 106–7; definition 39
formal and informal speech: reduction in 30–2, 32–3; speech accommodation 29–33
French 36, 83

Gerard, C. 36
gesture and prosody, as central components of discourse organization 108
Giles, H. 39
Gneezy, U. 60
Gussenhoven, C. 17–18, 73, 101
Gut, U. 13

Halle, M. 12

hearing-impaired infants 40
Henderson, S. 101
Hewings, M. 35
high-rising terminal 21–2; see also uptalk
Hirschberg, J. 18, 101, 103
Hoot, B. 12
Hualde, J.I. 10, 20

imaginary interlocutors, and accommodative speech 41–2
immersion in a TL environment, benefits of 5
individual variation, as future research direction 108
infant-directed speech (IDS) 39–43, 69, 73, 102, 106–7; definition 39
Instructed Second Language Acquisition (ISLA) 3, 37
intensity: as acoustic correlate of stress and focus 14–15; comparisons between SDS and conversation 68–9, *68*; discussion 70; as distinguishing factor in speech style 70, 86; individual variation 87–9, *88*, 90–1; meaning of 8; nativeness and 90–1; over time 92, 93; and placement of recording devices 53; variation across time 92, *93*, 98; see also articulation rate and intensityintonational diglossia 33
intonational phrases (IPs) 10, 19, 21, 70–1, 102
introverted personality, impact on pitch modulation 78, 102

Kempe, V. 41, 102
King, D. 101
Knapton, L. 41, 102
Kuhl, P.K. 40–1, 102
Kuhn, M.A. 60

L2 classrooms: complexity of prosody in 8–9; social roots of speech in 11; speech accommodation in discourse 33–7
L2 teachers: basis of knowledge about 47; classroom behaviours 1–2; roles played by 3; speech accommodation, variation 37–9

laboratory speech 19, 31–2, 36
Labov, W. 29–30
language grading 34–5, 74, 78, 98, 106
Latin American Spanish 19
Levy, E.T. 108
linear mixed effects models (LMEMs) 60–1
linguistic accommodations 2, 5, 40, 49, 103
Llurda, E. 107

Madrid Spanish 11, 14
McCune, K. 102
McNeill, D. 38
Medgyes, P. 37–8
motherese 4, 73, 102
Murakami, K. 36

narrow focus declaratives 11–13, 15–17, 32, 58, 76–7
nativeness: and articulation rate 13, *88*, 104; and intensity *88*, 90–1; as motivator for variation 106; and speech accommodation 37–8; of study participants 50
nativeness of L2 teachers: and speech rate during SDS 90; and student perceptions 38–9
naturalistic speech elicitation methodologies, importance of 107
near-native speaker teachers (NNSTs), advantages 37–8
Nibert, H.J. 10
Nuclear Stress Rule (NSR) 12

O'Rourke, E. 20, 36
Ortega-Llebaria, M. 14

paralinguistic information, examples of 8, 34, 36
participants and procedures: biographical data of participants **51**; coding of SDS and conversational speech tokens 57–9; curriculum **54**; data analysis 56, 59–61; data collection procedures 50–6; data input 56–9; description of participants 49–50; experience and educational background of participants **52**; extraction of SDS

Index

and conversational speech 56–7; follow-up interviews 55–6; in-class data collection 53–5; phrasal segmentation criteria 57; semi-structured focus group interviews 55
pedagogy, implications of findings for 105–7
Peninsular Spanish 19, 20
phonetic reduction *see* reduction
phonological words (PWs) 10
phrasal segmentation 22
phrase boundaries, pitch movement at 21–2
Pierrehumbert, J. 10
pitch: and communicative conventions 18; contours in SDS and conversation 71; F0 shift and 15, 17; as indicator of prominence 11; meaning of 8; phrasal boundary variation 20; speech rate and 13–14; in speech with imaginary interlocutors 41; statistical significance in the study 72–3; variation according to age and gender 17, 49; *see also* fundamental frequency (F0)
pitch accent, definition 10
pitch modulation 10, 82, 102, 104
pitch register 15, 17–19, 58
Praat acoustic analysis software 3, 49, 56–7
presentational focus 12
presentational speech 4, 86, 101
Prieto, P. 10, 14, 21
prosodic correlates: attention directing role 9–12; focus 11–12; intonation 10–11; stress 9
prosodic correlates of SDS: articulation rate and intensity 66–70; boundary pitch movement 79–84; F0 mean and range 70–4; F0 peak frequency and pre-nuclear F0 rise pattern 74–8
prosodic modifications: functions during IDS and FDS 41; research recommendations 109
prosodic prominence: definition 3; indicators 11; marking of 3, 14–16
prosodic variation: articulation rate across time in SDS 92; articulation rate and intensity by nativeness 88; BPM across time in SDS 95; changes over the academic semester 91–9; discussion 89–91; F0 mean across time in SDS 93; F0 range across time in SDS 94; intensity across time in SDS 93; pre-nuclear F0 rise patterns across time in SDS 95; study findings 87–9
prosody: components and purpose 2; during SDS 2–5; taco analogy 3

Quilis, A. 9, 31

Rao, R. 11–12, 21, 32, 36
reduction 11, 30–3, 97; examples of 31; extralinguistic factors 32–3; faster speech and 97; in FDS and IDS 40; formal vs informal speech 30–2; gender and age differences 32
research: methodology, implications of findings for 107; recommendations 108–9
research questions 48–9
Ritchie, S. 101
Roseano, P. 21

Samimy, R. 38
Scarborough, R. 41
sentence type, cues 20–1
Sessarego, S. 12
Sinclair, J.M. 34
Skidmore, D. 36
sociolinguistic observation, paradox of 30
Sosa, J.M. 10
Spanish Tones and Break Indices (Sp ToBI) 10, 109
speech accommodation: accommodative speech styles and contexts 39–43; concept of 29; evidence of pervasiveness in the L2 classroom 47; extralinguistic factors involved in reduction 32–3; foreigner-directed speech and infant-directed speech 40–1; formal and informal speech 29–33; implications, applied 42–3; interactional discourse in the L2 classroom 34–7; L2 classroom discourse 33–7; L2

speech accommodation *continued*
  teacher variation 37–9;
  methodological implications 41–2;
  nativeness and 37–8; phonetic
  reduction 30–2; prosody and
  intonation during SDS 35–7; student
  perspectives 38–9; teacher talk, roles
  of 34–5; theories 39–40
Speech Accommodation Theory (SAT)
  39
speech elicitation tasks *33*
speech melody: declarative intonation,
  variation in 19–21; phrase
  boundaries 21–2; pitch register
  17–19; role in directing attention
  17–22
speech rate *see* articulation rate
Stanley, P. 35
Stevenson, M. 35
stress: definition 9; use of in Spanish 9
stress and focus correlates: duration
  13–14; F0, 15–17; intensity 14–15
stressful emotions while teaching,
  physiological effects 35, 103
stress shift 12
Strik, H. 13

student-directed speech (SDS):
  characteristics 8; comparison with
  conversation 30, *67*, *68*, *71*, *72*, *75*,
  76, *79*, *80*, *88*; comparison with
  motherese 4; dual purpose 34;
  meaning of 3–4; prosody during
  2–5

teacher training, influence on prosodic
  behaviour during SDS 105–6
Tobin, K. 35, 101, 103
Toledo, G.A. 14
Tucker, B.V. 33

upstepping 20, 58, 71, 109; definition
  20
uptalk 21–2, 84, 103; definition 22

Vergara, D. 22
vocal anatomy 17, 49
vocal cords 15, 17–18

Walsh, S. 35
Warner, N. 33
Warren, P. 22
Willis, J. 34–5, 101

For Product Safety Concerns and Information please contact our EU representative GPSR@taylorandfrancis.com
Taylor & Francis Verlag GmbH, Kaufingerstraße 24, 80331 München, Germany

www.ingramcontent.com/pod-product-compliance
Lightning Source LLC
Chambersburg PA
CBHW070739230426
43669CB00014B/2516